CLEAN MAGIC

CLEAN MAGIC

The Essential Guide to a Sparkling Green Home

NANCY BIRTWHISTLE

ONE BOAT

First published 2026 by One Boat
an imprint of Pan Macmillan
The Smithson, 6 Briset Street, London EC1M 5NR
EU representative: Macmillan Publishers Ireland Ltd, 1st Floor,
The Liffey Trust Centre, 117–126 Sheriff Street Upper,
Dublin 1, D01 YC43

Associated companies throughout the world

ISBN 978-1-0350-8473-9

Copyright © Nancy Birtwhistle 2026

The right of Nancy Birtwhistle to be identified as the
author of this work has been asserted in accordance with
the Copyright, Designs and Patents Act 1988.

All rights reserved. No part of this publication may be reproduced,
stored in a retrieval system, or transmitted, in any form, or by any means
(including, without limitation, electronic, mechanical, photocopying, recording
or otherwise) without the prior written permission of the publisher.

Pan Macmillan does not have any control over, or any responsibility for,
any author or third-party websites (including, without limitation, URLs,
emails and QR codes) referred to in or on this book.

1 3 5 7 9 8 6 4 2

A CIP catalogue record for this book is available from the British Library.

Illustrations by Ruth Craddock

Typeset in Adobe Caslon Pro by Palimpsest Book Production Ltd, Falkirk, Stirlingshire

Printed and bound in the UK using 100% Renewable Electricity by CPI Group (UK) Ltd

This book contains the opinions and ideas of the author. It is intended to provide helpful
general information on the subjects that it addresses. Before following any instructions
outlined in this book, it is suggested that the reader undertakes a patch test to ensure
suitability and follows any relevant manufacturer or supplier guidelines. The publisher and
author disclaim all responsibility for damage, loss or injury of any kind resulting from tips
or instructions contained in this book. Handle materials with care. For use under
responsible adult supervision only. All necessary precautions should be taken.

This book is sold subject to the condition that it shall not, by way of
trade or otherwise, be lent, hired out, or otherwise circulated without
the publisher's prior consent in any form of binding or cover other than
that in which it is published and without a similar condition including this
condition being imposed on the subsequent purchaser. The publisher does not
authorize the use or reproduction of any part of this book in any manner
for the purpose of training artificial intelligence technologies or systems.
The publisher expressly reserves this book from the Text and Data Mining
exception in accordance with Article 4(3) of the European Union
Digital Single Market Directive 2019/790.

Visit **www.panmacmillan.com/bluebird** to read more about
all our books and to buy them.

To all who have joined me in deciding to go green – I think we are making a difference

CONTENTS

INTRODUCTION — 1

What does it mean to 'go green'? — 1

The essential green cleaning tool kit — 5

Kit and ingredients list — 6

What to use and where — 16

What to use and where by product — 21

MARKS AND STAINS — 39

Basic Magic — 43

The magic of Pure Magic — 48

Dry grease stain remover: Terre de Sommières — 56

Sticky stuff paste — 58

Dry cleaning foam — 59

Green bleach foam — 63

Cleaning patios, slippery steps, tarmac, pavers and decking — 68

Black spot lichen — 70

Cleaning a stone bird bath — 72

Clearing green algae and mould spots	73
Removing rust marks	74
Neutralizing stains	78
Pumice stone tricks	79
Marks on wood	87

DEEP CLEANS, BLOCKAGES AND REFRESHES — 93

Oven Magic	97
The big oven clean-up	101
Aluminium oven filters	107
The stinky sink	109
Avoid sink blockages	112
Slow-flowing sinks	115
Blocked toilets	118
Bye-bye fly	119

KITCHEN TIPS — 123

The big pantry clear out	129
Reusable piping bag	133
The stainless-steel pan	138
Seized washing soda (sodium carbonate)	143
Big fridge and freezer clean and tidy	145
Dishwasher detergent	151

GENERAL HOUSEHOLD TIPS — 155

No water waste	157
The bins	160

Mop cleaning	164
Lambswool fluffy	166
Sheepskin rugs	168
Window blinds cleaning	170
Preparing to decorate a room	172
The big car clean-up	173
Going on holiday cleaning checklist	178
Infused vinegar	181
Odourless surgical spirit/rubbing alcohol	184
Reed diffusers	184
Wild flower seed waste-paper gifts	187

CLOTHING AND LAUNDRY CARE 193

The big wardrobe refresh	196
Diatomaceous earth	198
Laundry fabric softener	200
Liquid laundry detergent	204
Wool/delicates detergent	206
Conker detergent mark II	211
Magic suds – ivy detergent	215
My yellow woollen coat – I washed it!	217
Tea towels	221
Hand-knitted dishcloths	224
Dye from jeans onto trainers	225
Avoid pilling of jumpers	226
Prevent and take action against clothes moths	228
Lavender wand	231

Easy breeze fabric spray	234
Nature's freebie: perfumed distilled ironing water	238
Fusty-smelling towels or clothing	240
Avoid faded lines on clothing	244
Bronzer and sun cream stains on clothing	245
Baby poosplosion	251
Slime stains	256
Brighten the bling!	258
Sandals and sliders	259
PERSONAL AND PETS	**261**
Liquid hand soap	263
Save your soap	266
Home-made deodorant	268
Body spray	274
Strengthen your tights	275
Pet-friendly cleaning	277
CONCLUSION	281
ACKNOWLEDGEMENTS	285
ABOUT THE AUTHOR	287
INDEX	289

INTRODUCTION

What does it mean to 'go green'?

When I look back to the early days and the very beginning of my green journey, I started off with a few simple swaps. First, I decided not to buy plastic cling film that I used just once, then I moved on a little and ditched single-use wipes and plastic bags, before progressing to never buying single-use plastic plates, cutlery and cups. Then I became more interested and motivated and the green wheel kept on turning.

Fast-forward ten years and by taking regular, very small steps the mission to save our planet has now gathered pace and evolved into a complete lifestyle change for me and so many like-minded people.

World leaders, organizations and governments may continue to pontificate and set targets and standards, but I remind myself that the greatest threat to our planet is the belief that someone else will save it. I can, in my little house, do something to help every single day.

I am often asked what motivates me to keep trying (and often failing) to achieve a satisfactory result to a question or cleaning problem that has presented itself. Sometimes I feel overwhelmed or disheartened, but I try not to be beaten. I keep going and then when I have a breakthrough and come up with a cleaning recipe, tip or solution and am able to share it amongst my now-large social media audience, I realize that this piece of work can then be multiplied by thousands of other little houses.

For those who say these actions are a drop in the ocean, my reply is always that an ocean is made up of many drops and our oceans are so precious! I firmly believe change can happen, is happening and will continue to gather pace. Even for the climate deniers out there, and setting global warming and climate change to one side for a moment, let us consider the facts and concentrate just on cleaning. The reverse labels on cleaning products are not fake news, many ingredients are toxic to aquatic life – it says so if you get your glasses on to read the tiny print. They may be harmful to pets, their synthetic perfumes will pollute the air we breathe inside our homes and their plastic containers will add to landfill or incineration and probably not be recycled, as we previously assumed. Then we have to think about the expense. Every 'single-use' plastic bottle or bag, along with the cost of its eventual disposal, every inch of shelf space in the supermarket, not forgetting the advertising, marketing and salaries of all of the staff involved in production. All those costs are added to the final retail price of that bottle of chemical cleaner! Thankfully, we have a way out of this – we can make our own cleaning products, so

we know what goes into them and can learn what works well for us in our own homes.

In my (and your) little kitchen we are the production line – no single-use spray bottles, tubs and containers, we reuse what we have. The marketing and advertising we excitedly do ourselves, as we tell more and more of our friends and family how effective, addictive and feelgood a 'green lifestyle' is.

As well as the brilliant cleaning results in our homes, the cost savings of 'going green' are, we realized in a very short time, tangible, as we happily skip up and down the cleaning aisle in the supermarket with an empty trolley.

Inside this book you'll find environmental and budget-friendly fixes for almost any problem around the home – from very stubborn stain removal to freshening stinky sinks and zero-effort slippery path and paver cleaning. These are easy and small changes that will make a big difference to your home and environment.

I began with a basket of simple natural ingredients and went on to make a selection of home-made cleaning products, sufficient to cover most jobs in and around my home. Yet, as more readers became convinced and committed to saving the planet, as well as seeing a significant reduction in their weekly household spend, questions were being posed about how to clean 'this or that' – items that, for me, so far hadn't been tackled.

My aim with this book, therefore, is to deal with the most-often-asked and specific issues head on. I have developed some new recipes and discovered new ingredients, and hopefully I can remedy your most challenging of cleaning problems.

Let us turn our backs on the expensive, brightly packaged, single-use, harmful products and learn a modern, new and natural way to clean. You'll not go back. That's a promise!

What's different about this book? My answer to that is, from the queries I receive there are still many cleaning stones to uncover. I get lots of questions from readers every day and those most frequently asked have been given their own dedicated space in this book. I am pleased to share the new recipes and natural ingredients I have discovered, and also a number of new uses for my much-loved tool kit – some of which continue to surprise me when I put them to the test.

In this book I give some time to the 'newbie greenies', those people really wanting to get started and who are trying so hard but don't know where to begin. I get lots of queries from those new to 'green cleaning' about what should be used and where, so I have included a table (see pages 36–37) that should help. Then, of course, there are the general household and laundry tips that I know so many crave.

The essential green cleaning tool kit

The satisfaction I always have on cleaning day (which for me is usually Saturday morning, when I go through the house from top to bottom) knowing my regime is now so very simple, cheap and effective is so rewarding. A few staple natural ingredients are absolutely all I ever need. My cupboard under the sink used to be packed full of brightly coloured spray bottles – one for each cleaning task. Totally unnecessary, chemical-heavy and costly. Now, my tidy little home-made caddy covers the lot!

Looking back to the time when I used to buy my cleaning products from the supermarket, so often I would see a brightly coloured flash over my favourite bottle, box of detergent or floor cleaner stating 'new and improved', and now I understand why. Some of my original recipes are approaching ten years in age, and over those years I have discovered myself that a tweak here or there has either improved performance, extended shelf life or made it go further. Those of you who have been on this journey with me for a while may recognize some of the recipes that I have improved here; in each case I have discovered new uses or have included some recommendations following user feedback.

Continuing to make living a sustainable lifestyle as easy, cheap and effective as possible has become a real passion for me, so I hope old and new readers alike can enjoy the 'Mark II' new and improved versions of these classics.

Kit and ingredients list

Not a day goes by when I don't receive a question from someone who's really excited to start out on their own green journey, but doesn't know what to do first. My advice is always to start slowly, with just one swap or one home-made cleaning product and, once this feels straightforward, move on.

I have had some people who have found themselves in a confused state. They have gone out to buy a shopping bag full of natural cleaning ingredients and then when confronted with a cleaning or stain problem have thrown everything at it and wondered why it didn't work. I have a recollection of someone with a badly stained toilet telling me they had given it washing soda, bicarbonate of soda, vinegar, washing-up liquid and then added tea tree oil for good measure – only to find after an initial fizz that nothing improved. My advice is: decide on something you want or need to tackle and rather than go out to buy the proprietary brands, have a go yourself using the specific advice in these pages. It may be laundry, it could be sink cleaning, or the toilet or the washing machine. Most recipes I have developed use the same or similar ingredients.

SIMPLE STARTER KIT

- Digital weighing scales
- Small funnel
- Spray bottles (choose glass or thoroughly wash and reuse plastic)

- Jars with lids

- Heatproof measuring jug

- Small whisk

- Cleaning cloths: I avoid buying microfibre cloths because of the microplastics that they emit, so I choose instead to upcycle old towels and pieces of cotton clothing. You will be amazed at how efficient and effective old t-shirts are as cleaning cloths. They don't fray and are just about the right thickness. Or, knit your own! See page 224.

- Eco-friendly washing-up liquid (choose an unperfumed brand without citrus scents)

- Distilled white vinegar

- Citric acid

- The three sodiums: green bleach (sodium percarbonate), bicarbonate of soda, washing soda (sodium carbonate).

Pure Magic

Pure Magic is a beast of a cleaner, and as time has gone on I have learned so much more about its magic powers. This recipe started life as a toilet cleaner – I christened it Toilet Magic – but as my green cleaning journey gathered pace I discovered it has so many other amazing uses. Pure Magic is a highly effective replacement for many toxic chemical products, ranging from limescale removers to metal rust, laundry stain and mould removers – I will cover all the many uses for it later. To avoid any pitfalls when making it, see below.

You will need

600ml (1 pint) heatproof measuring jug
digital weighing scales
small whisk or fork
small funnel (optional, but always helps)
400ml (14fl oz) glass bottle (or reuse a plastic one) with spray attachment

200g (7oz) citric acid
150ml (5fl oz) just-boiled water
20ml (¾fl oz) eco-friendly washing-up liquid
10 drops of essential oil (optional)

Place the citric acid in the heatproof measuring jug onto scales set to zero, then the rest of the weighing and mixing can be done in the one vessel. I find glass is best because then you can see what is going on.

Pour over the measure of just-boiled water straight from the kettle, then stir until completely dissolved and the solution is as clear as plain water. I get many questions from followers asking why their Pure Magic has crystallized; just one remaining tiny crystal, if not dissolved, will grow again, so spend time examining your solution to check that not one particle is left. If the solution has cooled and there are particles remaining, heat gently in the microwave or in a saucepan.

Once cool, add the washing-up liquid and, if using, the essential oil for perfume. Brightly coloured, branded chemical types of washing-up liquid may solidify the mix. Be sure, too, to use washing-up liquid or dish soap, not hand soap, as this may cause clumps. Leave the liquid in the jug to cool completely, uncovered, for a few hours, then transfer to a spray bottle – label it Pure Magic so that you don't get mixed up, and your cleaning can begin.

TOP TIP: When making up a bottle of Pure Magic (or any cleaning product), write the name in bold letters on one side, then on the reverse, in smaller print, write out the ingredients. This saves so much time when you need a refill. For example: 200g (7oz) citric acid, 150ml (5fl oz) boiling water, 20ml (¾fl oz) eco-friendly washing-up liquid, 10 drops of essential oil. There are glass writing pens on the market that can be used to write on the glass, then just leave them for an hour or so to dry before following the manufacturer's instructions for placing into a cold oven, which is usually heated for about an hour. Turn the oven off, leave the glass to cool and the writing is fixed for good.

All-purpose spray cleaner

One of my first ever recipes and still often my 'go-to' for daily cleaning tasks. I cover its many uses throughout the book.

You will need

300ml (10fl oz) spray bottle
digital weighing scales
small funnel (optional)

60ml (2fl oz) white vinegar (or infused vinegar see pages 181–182)
150ml (5fl oz) water
40ml (1¼fl oz) surgical spirit (rubbing alcohol) or cheap vodka
10 drops of essential oil (optional)

Place the empty spray bottle onto weighing scales, with a small funnel in the neck to prevent spills, if you like. Set the scales to zero then pour the vinegar into the bottle. Set the scales to zero again, add the water, then set to zero and add the surgical spirit followed by essential oil for perfume, if using. Fix the spray nozzle, give it a shake and it is good to go. I use it most days around my house.

TOP TIP: All of the cleaning recipes can be made in bulk in larger containers and spray bottles – the sizes given are those that are convenient for me.

Cream cleaner

So many uses! Simple to make, yet far from simple as a cleaning product when it comes to its adaptability and capability. My non-acidic cream cleaner will make you so pleased you decided to 'go green'.

You will need

500ml (17fl oz) glass jar or tub with screw top
digital weighing scales
small spoon

200g (7oz) bicarbonate of soda
70ml (2¼fl oz) vegetable glycerine
30ml (1fl oz) eco-friendly washing-up liquid (non-citrus-scented)
a few drops of essential oil (optional, non-acidic or citrus scented)

I stand an empty jar onto my digital weighing scales, set to zero, then add the bicarb, reset to zero again and add the glycerine, reset to zero again and add the washing-up liquid. Add a few drops of essential oil, if using, then stir everything together with a small spoon until smooth and thick (about the consistency of thick cream). Screw the lid on and it is good to go.

Cream cleaner FAQs

My cream cleaner has been found to have so many uses. If you are new to my recipes, I have listed below the questions I am most often asked.

My cream cleaner feels chalky, why isn't it smooth?

In the UK, the difference between bicarbonate of soda and baking powder can cause confusion and create problems when it comes to making cream cleaner. Choose bicarbonate of soda only for the recipe because, unlike baking powder, it doesn't contain acid in the form of cream of tartar, which once moistened creates bubbles. When used in baking, it's these bubbles that expand to make cakes rise. Using baking powder rather than bicarbonate of soda will do the same thing in the jar – a chemical reaction will occur, causing the cream to bubble and expand but then separate and turn coarse and gritty.

Shall I perfume my cream cleaner?

It happened to me too. When I first embarked on my 'green journey' I needed the perfumes. I realized I had come to associate clean with a pleasing scent. Gradually I have become less dependent and can happily live without perfume in certain cleaning products. For example, I still perfume my fabric softener to give a lasting scent to my laundry, but I realized adding perfume to laundry detergent is pointless. I will come back to that later.

Be careful with cream cleaner. For the same reason that baking powder can cause problems for cream cleaner, so can essential oils. I have had countless people tell me that their cream cleaner has gone hard, has separated, or at worst gone solid in the jar. On further discussion the reason has been the addition of acidic essential oil or citrus-perfumed washing-up liquid. The obvious ones to avoid are the citrus scents – lemon, orange, etc. – but lavender can also sometimes cause separation. Choose unperfumed washing-up liquid. My advice – either leave out the perfume altogether or use a non-acidic oil such as sandalwood (my perfume of choice for cream cleaner) or myrtle.

Basic Magic

This is a new recipe that has quickly found a place in my essential tool kit. See pages 43–48 for its main uses and for the recipe.

Magic Mixers

As my green journey has gathered pace I found myself wanting to improve old recipes and at the same time introduce new ones. I needed a 'mixer' – an ingredient that would emulsify oil and water so that I could introduce natural essential oil scents into recipes ensuring the perfume mixed in rather than simply floated on the top.

Below are natural emulsifiers that work perfectly, ensuring perfume in every spray, dose or application.

Polysorbate 80 – a new ingredient and a bit of a mouthful, so I call it Magic Mixer. As with anything in life, the more one knows, the more there is to know, and this little bottle of plant-based emulsifier has improved a number of my cleaning and household recipes and enabled me to introduce new ones because it has the ability to mix oil and water together.

I have read that it is used widely in cosmetics as well as some foods, and is vegan. It comes from sorbitan, a plant-derived sugar, alcohol and oleic acid that can be sourced from plants like coconut or sunflowers. Some are derived from palm oil, though it is easy to find palm-free products.

Honey and or liquid glucose – another amazing quality of natural honey is its ability to emulsify water and oil, so if you have reservations about Polysorbate 80 or find it difficult to source then a drop of honey (or, for smaller quantities, a tiny drizzle off a teaspoon and then eat the rest!) added to the products will magically emulsify the two. I use clear runny honey but liquid glucose available from the supermarket on the baking aisle will also do the job and, unlike honey, is suitable for vegans.

Use these Magic Mixers a few drops at a time in recipes where appropriate. I have decided it is worth emulsifying certain products though I don't think it is absolutely essential if you are just starting out. I've used a Magic Mixer in my reed diffuser recipe, fabric softener, Easy Breeze fabric spray, moth mist, spray deodorant, body mist and general polish to date.

General polish

This very effective polish has so many uses – on wood especially, but also stainless steel, and I use it to give leather shoes a quick wipe over when I am in a rush. With a few drops of our new ingredient, Magic Mixer, it is now fully emulsified, so there's no separation and no need to shake it every time.

You will need

spray bottle

50ml (1¾fl oz) sunflower, vegetable or baby oil (the thinnest, cheapest oil that you have)
30ml (1fl oz) white vinegar
20–30 drops of essential oil (I like to use lavender)
Magic Mixer (10 drops polysorbate 80 or 1 drop honey or glucose)

Simply measure the ingredients into the bottle, shake to emulsify and it is ready to go.

I always spray this onto a dry cloth, not onto the item to be cleaned, in order to avoid over spraying and for a more even application.

What to use and where

I receive many messages from people, particularly welcome 'green newbies', who feel overwhelmed. There is so much information, so many new things to think about that have never been considered before – in the form of acids and alkaline – and there seem to be so many recipes. I am often asked for lists of 'what to use and where', so I thought I would go room by room with separate sections on relevant products.

Kitchen

WORK SURFACES

All-purpose spray cleaner and a damp or dry cloth for a quick spray and wipe. Never use Pure Magic because it will dry sticky.

GRANITE, STONE, SLATE AND UNTREATED WOOD

Do not use acidic cleaners because they can damage these materials. Use my cream cleaner and buff with a dry cloth or use a spray of Basic Magic, though don't overdo it because it can leave a chalky film which will show up on dark surfaces.

OVENS

See the Big Oven Clean Up on pages 101–108 and Oven Magic on pages 97–101.

GLASS INDUCTION HOB

Wipe down after use with a warm, damp cloth. Use all-purpose spray cleaner and a dry cloth to polish and remove any water marks.

For badly stained glass hobs, use my cream cleaner and a dry cloth.

For burnt-on plastic, heat the hob on the lowest setting until just hot then turn off the power. Use a wooden spoon or spatula to gently rub away and remove the softened plastic. Once the surface has cooled down, use my cream cleaner and a dry cloth to remove any residue, then shine and polish using my all-purpose spray cleaner.

CUPBOARDS AND DOORS

These come in many types, so choose whichever product works best for you. Always test a small area first to see which product gives the best result. All-purpose spray cleaner, Basic Magic or my cream cleaner – I use all three. Try all-purpose spray cleaner for fingerprints, Basic Magic for tough jobs (the tops of cupboards, for example) and cream cleaner for bare wood.

COOKER ALUMINIUM FILTERS

Never use washing soda because it will permanently tarnish the metal. Use a green bleach soak – see pages 107–108 for details.

STAINLESS-STEEL COOKER HOODS

My general polish works very well when sprayed onto a dry cloth rather than directly onto the surface to be cleaned. It will cut through grease, leaving the stainless steel shiny and smear-free.

KITCHEN SINK

See the kitchen sink cleaning on pages 109–111.

General cleaning

STAINLESS STEEL

Use a sprinkle of bicarbonate of soda on its own, or use cream cleaner or all-purpose spray cleaner for daily use. Pure Magic and an old toothbrush will dissolve limescale around taps and on drainers – spray on, then scrub with an old toothbrush, leave for 15 minutes and rinse well.

CERAMIC AND COMPOSITE SINKS

If acidic cleaners are not recommended for your ceramic or composite sink, use cream cleaner or Basic Magic. For very stubborn stains, wet the area, sprinkle over a teaspoon of green bleach (see page 30 for more on this ingredient), brush it in and leave to whiten. I make this a last-thing-at-night job. Sprinkle over the green bleach then rinse the next morning. For a slow-flowing sink, see pages 115–117. For a stinky sink, see pages 109–111.

COMPOSITE DOORS

Try cream cleaner to restore dull and stained composite front doors. Many have marvelled at the results. Use on a dry cloth and see the difference.

STAINED TOILET SEATS

For those toilet seats that are permanent and fixed and can't be easily unclipped and soaked in washing soda, try using Oven Magic (see page 97). With the seat in the up position, paint on the gloop and leave it to soak and work its magic on tough, unsightly areas. A one-hour soak should be sufficient, then wipe clean.

FLOORS

For tiled floors dilute 2 tablespoons of my all-purpose floor cleaner in a bucket of hot water. Simply combine the following ingredients:

- 200ml (7fl oz) white vinegar (see infused vinegar on page 181)
- 50ml (1¾fl oz) eco-friendly washing-up liquid
- 20–30 drops of essential oil (orange and lemon are my favourites)

Many followers have used this mix diluted to half-strength in floor-cleaning machines.

See the bodywork solution used for car cleaning on page 174, too, as many have used a half-strength solution of this to clean very neglected soft tops on cars.

For a non-acidic floor cleaner and for grout cleaning, see Basic Magic for floors on page 23, and use for encaustic floor tiles, slate, stone, laminated wood and natural wood.

Living room

MIRRORS AND GLASS

All-purpose spray cleaner and a dry cloth.

WOODEN FURNITURE

General polish.

CARPET STAINS

For stains from the likes of lipstick, make-up or biro, try a pad dipped in surgical spirit.

For stains from grease, oil, chocolate or a fat spill, try a pad dipped in Basic Magic.

AIR FRESHENERS

See my Easy Breeze fabric spray, page 234, and reed diffusers, page 184.

What to use and where by product

Many followers will have their own favourite uses for my homemade products, but for those unsure of what to use and where, here is a simple list.

Once you embrace this new cleaning lifestyle change you will get to know the recipes and you can decide for yourself what to try. You will be delighted with the results. Most products have more than one use, and that is what is so fantastic about making your own. You will see from the list below that more than one product can be used for the same job – I certainly ring the changes. For example, armed with my carrying caddy of products when I go upstairs to clean the bathroom, I may find myself dipping in and out using various products, but as an aid, the information below should be useful.

Basic Magic

Non-acidic, cheap to make and handy to always have mixed and ready.

GOOD ALL-ROUNDER

Use to clean baths and sinks, or dilute it and use as a floor cleaner or a grease blaster on oven hobs, tile grouting, or as a prewash stain remover for collars and cuffs. Can be used straight from the bottle or as a spray. Has been used to successfully remove black oil, slime and sun cream from carpets and upholstery. Safe on clothing fabrics (though not on silk or wool), wood, granite, stone and encaustic tiles, though it can leave a chalky film if not wiped clean. One person I remember sent me great before and after photos when she cleaned a whole caravan using Basic Magic.

ACRYLIC BATH

I prefer Basic Magic for my acrylic bath; 1–2 tablespoons poured into the bath then used with a slightly dampened cloth cleans it like nothing else. A quick rinse and the finish is smooth, shiny and free of any soap scum.

TILE GROUT

Basic Magic and an old toothbrush or nail brush for tile grout I have now discovered works the best.

STAINS FROM GREASE

Oil, chocolate and/or scuffs on walls, carpets, shoes and upholstery. Spot clean by using a clean cotton pad dipped in Basic Magic, then dab at the affected area to remove stains. Remember to always test a small area first.

LAUNDRY

Grubby collars, cuffs, body odour stains and other odours – a spray onto stained laundry before washing often saves having to presoak the item.

PVC CLEANING

Spray directly onto a surface and wipe clean with a damp cloth.

STONES

Granite, marble or stone can be cleaned of algae, dirt and some lichens without fear of damage to the stone. Use for stone and concrete bird baths, garden ornaments and paved areas. Use diluted with hot water to scrub pavers, then rinse after use.

FLOORS

For wooden, stone and slate floors my cleaning product of preference is now Basic Magic. I use 2–3 tablespoons of Basic Magic diluted in a bucket of warm water to use with a mop as a floor cleaner. It can be used along with green bleach (see page 30) for very tough floor-cleaning jobs on tiles. Add 1 teaspoon of green bleach and 2–3 tablespoons of Basic Magic to a bucket of very hot water. Spray floor and wall tile grouting with Basic Magic, then scrub with an old sink, nail or toothbrush and your grouting will come up an absolute treat. I have lost count of the number of 'before and after' grouting pics I have seen and, being non-acidic, it will not damage any tiles or their grouting. Remember to wipe down well, especially dark-coloured tiles and grouting, because any residue will leave a chalky film.

Not for use on aluminium, because sodium carbonate can tarnish the metal.

All-purpose spray cleaner

This is a very popular cleaning product, though I have had messages from people either saying they don't like the smell of the vinegar or they don't like the clinical odour from the surgical spirit. If this is a problem to you (I love the smell of both), we can get around it.

Vinegar can be infused with lemon or orange peel to remove its pungent odour (see page 181), or both vinegar and surgical spirit can be sourced odour-free.

This handy spray is cheap to make, naturally anti-bac and very effective – I use it most days to wipe down before and after cooking or baking, and it leaves my induction hob gleaming too. It cleans without leaving smears or residue, dries to a shine and insects hate it!

KITCHEN SURFACES

Just spray and wipe over with a dry cloth.

THE SINK, TOILET SEAT, TILES

Spray then wipe with a damp cloth to leave surfaces clean as a whistle.

MIRRORS AND GLASS

Spray, then polish using a dry cloth – mirrors and glass will be cleaned immediately with no smears.

INSECTS

Spray on surfaces and floors to repel crawling insects, especially ants. A quick spray onto arms and legs before going out in the evening keeps biting insects away – and insects love me! As with anything going onto your skin, it's best to do a patch test on a small area first to check for sensitivity, and always avoid spraying on any broken skin.

MULTI-SURFACE CLEANER

You can use this as a 'spray and go' daily surface cleaner on many items. Spray and wipe with a dry cloth on kitchen and bathroom sinks and taps without the need for water, and kitchen and bathroom sanitaryware will be gleaming. It also works well on white furniture, glass-topped tables, gloss paintwork, PVC, kitchen shelves and skirting boards.

ACIDIC STAINS

A quick spritz directly onto certain stains on clothing before washing – try on fruit juice, food stains and wine (not grease, make-up, oil or sun cream). See cream cleaner (page 11) for greasy stains. Try to think it through – for example, acid on acid; the vinegar in all-purpose (acid) is good for treating acidic stains in fruits, wine and certain foods. If in doubt, try it out! If it doesn't work, we have something else that will.

Not to be used on natural granite, stone, slate or marble because it can damage them. Use non-acidic Basic Magic (see page 43), as all-purpose spray cleaner is acidic.

Pure Magic

Queen of the Green Clean and it has so many uses. My natural cleaner that does the job is economical and an eco alternative to harmful chlorine bleach. The main ingredient is citric acid, a natural cleaning product that will kill bacteria, mould and mildew, and dissolve limescale, water stains, calcium deposits and rust.

As Pure Magic is acidic, it is not recommended for use on granite or marble, stone or slate and some composite sinks (see manufacturer's instructions). I use it on my stainless-steel and chrome taps to remove water stains and limescale build-up. Before using, always test a small area first. I had one follower who managed to remove the shiny coating from a metal (looking) soap holder, only to find it was plastic-coated with a shiny finish.

Remember, Pure Magic is a beast of a cleaner but it is not designed for use on work surfaces. So many people message me to say that their Pure Magic has dried leaving a sticky residue. It will do this if it is not rinsed off well, and for this reason it is better to use my 'spray and go' all-purpose spray cleaner instead.

TOILET CLEANING

Use daily as a spray, brush and flush. For a major toilet deep clean, and for the toughest of toilet stains, see pages 51–54.

LIMESCALE REMOVAL

Tough limescale can be unsightly, corrosive and can harbour germs. Use Pure Magic around taps in baths and sinks. Spray onto the affected areas, brush with an old toothbrush, leave to soak for a minimum of 10 minutes, then rinse off. Very heavily scaled areas may need a repeated session or to be left to soak overnight. Again, if in doubt always test a small area first.

DESCALE KETTLE

Boil a kettle of water, stand it in the sink, then add 4 tablespoons of Pure Magic and see the limescale dissolve away. If you don't have Pure Magic made up and ready, add 80g (3oz) citric acid crystals to the kettle of boiled water and this will remove the thickest limescale.

Once the descale is complete the solution will still have some umph, so rather than pour the solution straight down the sink, pour it down the toilet. Don't flush, and leave it as long as is practical in order to give the bowl a quick clean. Waste not, want not!

DISSOLVES RUST ON FABRICS, PATHS, SINKS AND GARDEN TOOLS

See pages 74–77.

LAUNDRY STAIN REMOVAL

Use to remove curry, soy sauce, turmeric, mustard, tomato pasta sauce, baby poo, sun cream,

orange juice, melon and other fruit and veg stains – and to whiten whites.

Be careful, though. Use Pure Magic in cold water as a soak for stains – don't spray directly onto fabrics because it can bleach colours or leave a yellow mark on whites. For a more gentle prewash spray, see my all-purpose spray cleaner (page 10).

ALGAE REMOVER

Use in greenhouses, on boats, sun parasols, garden ornaments, bird baths and outdoor furniture. Pure Magic plus sunshine will do a great cleaning job on algae-covered and water-stained items. I have found the best results when I spray, brush using an old sink brush with soapy water, then rinse using clean water. Leave in full sunshine to complete the clean and the drying.

PURE MAGIC GEL

Use to clean areas where the product needs to remain and not run off, such as under the toilet rim, on shower runners, sink stains, rust marks on surfaces and fabrics (see page 50 for recipe).

PURE MAGIC FLUSH

Use to clean the cistern and water flow in areas you cannot get to (see pages 52–53 for recipe). *Not to be used on natural stone, wood, marble, slate and granite.*

Over to you!

I have had so many messages over the years from readers who have either inherited a heavily scaled granite kitchen sink, bathroom or shower or have developed rust stains and/or limescale on slate, stone and marble. What should be done to clean it up?

As we know, limescale is unsightly, can be corrosive and can harbour germs. Acidic cleaners are not recommended for regular use because they can damage materials. Faced with the same dilemma I would use Pure Magic as a 'one off' – it will whizz through that limescale and remove it quickly. The important thing is to rinse it off thoroughly using hot water and to not use it repeatedly. I always suggest to people that they make their own decision and always test a small area first. Needless to say, many come back to say things have cleaned up a treat, and for the future a regular clean down using either my cream cleaner or Basic Magic will prevent a huge problem further down the line.

Cream cleaner

Easy to make, simply mixed in a jar, and it has so many uses. This is a safe cleaner, and being non-acidic and non-scratch it will effectively clean so many items.

GOOD ALL-ROUNDER

Use to remove grease stains (even those already washed in) from clothing. Remove sticky label residue and stains from clothing. Cleans trainers and sports shoes. Use as a cleaner in bathrooms on sinks and baths, and as an oven and hob cleaner. Also good for outdoor plastic furniture and PVC window frames and doors. Being non-acidic and non-scratch, you can use it to remove minor scuffs and scrapes and bug stains on cars. Use to restore sparkling clarity to car headlights. So many people have told me they have saved money on specialist car headlight cleaning products. A wipe with my cream cleaner on a dry cloth does the job. Use to clean unvarnished and natural wood using a dry cloth. Stained induction hobs can be cleaned using cream cleaner and a dry cloth. Used with a dry cloth it will remove tarnish from silver items.

STICKY PLASTIC

Old plastic and silicone can become sticky over time, and many hairbrush and tool handles, including children's toys and hand grips on machinery and bicycles, have been thoroughly cleaned and brought back to life.

Green bleach (sodium percarbonate)

For those just starting out on their green journey this may be a completely new product. At the time of writing, I am not certain that any supermarket in the UK stocks this amazing ingredient, though eco shops will stock it and supermarkets in Europe have it on their shelves. When I started out on my journey I had to import it, whereas now I believe it is manufactured in the UK, and I hope that very soon UK supermarkets will have it on their shelves too.

We know and understand that chlorine bleach is harmful to the environment, gives off toxic fumes and will leave stains on clothing, fabrics and other items if not handled carefully. Thankfully, green bleach is eco-friendly, does the same job and is far more forgiving. I get lots of questions because many believe green bleach (like chlorine) will stain coloured fabrics. Green bleach is not brutal like chlorine and I have found that it can be used safely to remove stains even at low temperatures. It is activated quickly in boiling water, though it can be used with cold. It remains effective for around 6–7 hours, after which time it decomposes into soda ash, water and oxygen. No wonder we love it. It is a little more expensive than the rest of our tool kit, though a little goes a long way.

Do not mix green bleach (alkaline) with acids (i.e. Pure Magic or all-purpose spray cleaner). I remember one person messaging me to say that she thought she would give her Pure Magic some extra power by adding green bleach and then use it as a toilet cleaner. The result – the two opposing chemicals reacted together, producing lots of foam and bubbles and a huge mess, which resulted in no cleaning power at all. Remember to stick to acids with acids and alkaline with alkaline.

WASHING MACHINE

Use as an ingredient to remove mould in the washing machine that may have developed on the rubber seal (see recipe on page 66).

SINK

Some composite sink manufacturers may state that acidic cleaners are not advisable. At bedtime, wet the sink with cold water, sprinkle over a teaspoon of green bleach and leave overnight. The sink will be gleaming white the next day without the need for any scrubbing or harmful acidic products.

TEAPOT, STAINED CUPS AND CLOTHS

One teaspoon will do the lot. Once a week, I add a teaspoon of green bleach to my teapot with its mesh strainer in place (which was always impossible to clean), top up with boiling water and all is white and bright again in about 15 minutes. Pour the solution into any stained cups for 10–15 minutes, then pour the whole lot into a bowl in the sink containing your stained dishcloth. It may be expensive, but I make it work its socks off for me.

GRANITE, STONE AND SLATE WORKTOPS

Many people who have asked for advice about how to remove stains from granite and marble have had success with green bleach. Acidic cleaners are not recommended for use on granite and most natural stone, and I have had many questions from people stumped as to what to do with curry stains, wine stains and coffee and teacup rings that have continued to be stubborn even after trying my cream cleaner and a dry cloth. Try this: simply wet the area around the stain with just a tablespoon of water or a spray, then add half a teaspoon of green bleach. Work it in using a cotton bud or small brush and leave it to do its job. Stains should dissolve within an hour or so. No acids are involved and no harm will come to the surface.

DENTAL RETAINERS

Stained dental retainers can be returned to clean and clear using green bleach. Add half a teaspoon of green bleach to a mug or cup, then pour over 150ml (5½fl oz) of boiling water. Allow the solution to cool down to hand hot, then add the retainers and leave to soak for a few hours. Rinse well after the soak. Badly stained retainers may need a second application.

General polish

I always spray it directly onto a dry cloth to use on wood, stainless steel, leather shoes and bags – it also brightens up my leather sofa.

Washing soda (sodium carbonate)

Where would we be without washing soda? Natural, anti-bacterial grease-busting, odour-eliminating, a water softener and a good all-rounder. I use it as an ingredient in various recipes, on its own, dissolved into a liquid or sprinkled just as it is.

LAUNDRY

Living in a hard-water area, I use washing soda in every wash load to soften the water, dissolve stains and prevent any limescale build-up in my machine. Washing soda is inexpensive, especially if bought in bulk, and I use it routinely as a pre-soak for stains and odours. Smelly sports kits and gym clothes can be stripped of their odours using a tepid overnight soak prior to washing. As an aside, many 'slime' stains have been resolved using a washing soda pre-soak.

OVENS

Washing soda is a very effective degreaser and is used in Oven Magic (see page 99 for recipe). Washing soda in this thick, gloopy form will stay where it is and work at dissolving even the worst burnt-on oven spills and splashes.

STONE CLEANER

A great non-acidic cleaner – washing soda in liquid form will tackle those materials where acid cleaners are not recommended – such as granite, stone and slate (see page 44 for recipe).

Surgical spirit

Used on its own and as an ingredient in mixes, surgical spirit can sort many problems.

A stubborn stain can be removed quickly using a clean cotton pad dipped in surgical spirit and would be my first suggestion for lipstick, lily pollen, make-up, nail varnish, shoe polish, paint, tar, ink and biro on upholstery, clothing or carpets. I use a permanent marker to label my boxes, glass jars and bags for the freezer. Once used, the permanent marker can be removed using a pad dipped in surgical spirit, then washed and used again for something else.

Just a note about permanent ink and marker pens – they tend to do what they say and if not tackled quickly, and certainly if they get washed in, they can be troublesome.

RECIPE	WASHING SODA	BICARB. OF SODA	GREEN BLEACH	CITRIC ACID	WHITE VINEGAR	ECO W. LIQUID	VEG. GLYCERIN
Pure Magic				Y		Y	
Pure Magic gel				Y		Y	
Pure Magic flush				Y		Y	
Oven Magic	Y					Y	
Basic Magic	Y					Y	
All purpose spray					Y		
Cream cleaner		Y				Y	Y
Polish					Y		
Easy breeze							
Green bleach foam			Y				Y
Wool & delicates detergent							Y
Laundry detergent	Y					Y	
Fabric softener					Y		Y
Floor cleaner (all purpose)					Y	Y	
Dry cleaning foam	Y	Y	Y			Y	
Sticky stuff remover		Y					
Dishwasher detergent		Y	Y	Y	Y		
Deodorants							
Liquid hand soap		Y				Y	Y
Body spray							

XANTHAN GUM	SURGICAL SPIRIT	ESSENT. OILS	SOAP FLAKES	OIL	MAGIC MIXER	VODKA	WITCH HAZEL	SALT
		Y						
Y								
		Y						
Y								
		Y						
	Y	Y						
		Y						
		Y		Y	Y			
		Y			Y	Y		
Y								
			Y					
			Y					
		Y						
		Y						
				Y				
		Y			Y		Y	Y
Y		Y	Y					
		Y			Y		Y	

MARKS AND STAINS

Marks and stains on laundry, walls, furniture, carpets and clothing continue to present themselves, and just when I think I have tackled every possible problem, along comes someone with a new challenge. I always hope to get there in the end, and I urge you to do the same. Sometimes a stain, particularly an old one of unknown origin, will put us through our paces, but usually there is a way around it.

When I consider the money and time I spent on proprietary products, including detergents, sprays and rub-on sticks that promised to dissolve even the most stubborn stains but then often never did, I'm horrified. Those stained items ended up in the pile of working and gardening clothes.

I have even had many a query from those who have gone to the expense of purchasing stain-removing products only to find they have left their own set of new stains – which, thankfully, natural remedies have often gone on to solve. Cleaning magic at its very best.

This chapter discusses my favourite recipes along with an explanation on how they can be used. You will see that one product can sort a number of problems, and this is the beauty of 'going green' – less storage space is needed on your cleaning shelf.

Basic Magic

My need to write recipes and introduce solutions has always come about due to a pressing cleaning problem in my own home. However, once green cleaning started to gather pace and more people were getting involved, more questions were presented. What was apparent was that my handy sprays were acidic, being made using either vinegar, as in my all-purpose spray cleaner (see page 10) or citric acid for Pure Magic (see page 7). While I was happy using them around my own home, there were people who wanted something non-acidic to use on stone, granite and slate – those natural materials that can easily be damaged by acid.

I needed a non-acidic, non-scratch, gentle but effective cleaner that wouldn't cost the Earth (double meaning there!). I wasn't sure of a name for this one and asked my followers to decide. After a poll, Basic Magic was suggested, which I thought fitted the bill perfectly. A little explanation and science crash course-coming up.

In chemistry, pH is a figure expressing the acidity or alkalinity of a solution on a scale; 7 is neutral, less than 7 indicates acidity (e.g. vinegar, lemon juice, citric acid), and higher values are more alkaline. Base in chemistry indicates a pH of more than 7 (e.g. sodium carbonate, sodium bicarbonate, sodium percarbonate). As this cleaner is alkaline and a type of base, Basic Magic fitted perfectly.

You will need

    digital weighing scales
    small bowl
    500ml (17fl oz) heatproof jug
    small whisk
    funnel
    300ml (10fl oz) spray bottle or bottle with screw top

    50g (2oz) washing soda (sodium carbonate)
    200ml (7fl oz) just-boiled water
    2 tbsp unperfumed eco-friendly washing-up liquid
    a few drops of essential oil (optional, no citrus scents,
        sandalwood works well)

Weigh the washing soda into the small bowl and put to one side.

Place the jug onto your scales and set to zero. Pour in the just-boiled water. Add 1 tablespoon of washing soda at a time, stirring between each addition using the whisk until the crystals are completely dissolved and the mix looks cloudy but without sediment. Then add the washing-up liquid and a few drops of essential oil for perfume, if using. Stir and leave to cool completely.

This cleaner is very effective, cheap to make and an excellent grease-buster.

Use as a pre-wash laundry treatment to remove Calpol, chocolate, greasy collars and cuffs. It is a must for grouting on floors and wall tiles. See flow chart on pages 36–37 for where to use.

If this is used liberally to spray and wipe – particularly on dark surfaces – a chalky residue can remain, so a good wipe down after application is necessary. For a 'spray and go' cleaner, choose my all-purpose spray cleaner on page 10.

Basic Magic tips

Be mindful that acid and alkaline don't mix, and just as bicarbonate of soda and lemon juice come together and create a fizz as they cancel each other out, the same will happen with this cleaner if acids are introduced. I have had many cries for help from people who have explained they followed the recipe to the letter but the next day the solution had solidified in the bottle or had fizzed up and out through the spray. The use of an unscented, eco-friendly washing-up liquid is essential – lemon, clementine, grapefruit are acidic and it has also been discovered that these, along with lavender and pomegranate scents, can create a problem. For a free-flowing, non-clumping solution, choose unscented eco-friendly washing-up liquid and a non-acidic essential oil for perfume, or leave the perfume out altogether. In the early days I was confused myself when one batch of cream cleaner remained thick and luscious yet my next batch separated, felt gritty and ultimately set into a solid lump in the jar. I then came to understand that introducing anything but unperfumed washing-up liquid was causing a problem, as can even a tiny drop of acidic essential oil for perfume.

I spent some time researching essential oil acidity levels, and while lemon and orange, etc., are obviously citrus and acidic, I hadn't realized that lavender and eucalyptus too were at the wrong side of the pH level for my non-acidic cleaners. I now routinely use sandalwood, which doesn't clump. It is possible to check the pH of essential oils via a Google search before taking the plunge. You are looking for a pH of 7 or higher – peppermint is 8 (good), rose is neutral (good), lavender is 6 and acidic (good for Pure Magic and all-purpose spray cleaner but not for Basic Magic or cream cleaner). Basic Magic can also crystallize if it gets too cold. Standing it in a warm room will bring it back to normal in an hour or so.

Use Basic Magic as a spray or straight from a screw-top bottle, whichever works best for you. When I first developed this recipe I was intending to use Basic Magic as a handy spray. It will spray, though I found that the nozzle can block and I was forever rinsing to free it up.

I then decided to make life much easier and I now make it and store in a screw-top bottle, then I decant it into a spray bottle to use for specific, difficult-to-reach areas. As it is so inexpensive to make, I am not concerned that I use rather more from the bottle than I would if it was in spray form. Winding the clock back, of course, back in the day I don't recall any cleaning products being available in spray bottles. There were tubs of polish, shakers of bathroom dry cleaner (probably bicarb) and bottles of chlorine bleach.

With Basic Magic, I pour a little either onto the item to be cleaned (greasy hob, kitchen cupboard top or bath/sink), then use a cloth or old sink brush to work it in. For vertical applications (tile grouting, etc.) or as a pre-wash stain remover I will use my spray bottle to get it right where it needs to be, then in the case of tile grouting, I use an old toothbrush to finish the cleaning. For laundry, I pop the sprayed items directly into the washing machine drum.

This great little budget cleaner can be used as follows:

Spray or use from a bottle with a damp cloth on baths and sanitaryware – it's especially ideal for acrylic and plastic baths, which can build up a thin layer of almost-invisible, rough-feeling soap scum. They come up an absolute treat, as the surface returns to a smooth, shiny finish.

Spray or use from the bottle on wall and floor tiles and grouting. Scrub with an old nail or sink brush for an instant clean. As it is non-acidic, it won't damage or weaken materials.

Soak a clean cotton pad with Basic Magic and dab at stains on carpets, shoes, clothing and upholstery to slowly and carefully remove grease stains. Always test a small area first.

A spray onto dried bird poo that's left to soak for a few minutes will soften and remove the most stubborn stains from house paintwork, PVC and cars.

Spritz onto make-up and sun-cream stains before popping into the washing machine, though difficult stains may need my 'sun cream treatment' – see pages 248–250.

Safe to use on composite sinks as a daily sink clean.

Effective on tea and coffee stains on cups and teapots. Spray into the cup and use an exfoliating glove to rub around the stubborn stains to lift them quickly and effortlessly.

Spray onto the rubber seal on automatic washing machines to remove soap scum stains. See page 63 for washing machine mould treatment.

Use a spray around the seals on dishwashers to remove any build-up of yucky brown debris that collects in the corners and around the door seals.

Basic Magic floor cleaner

A non-acidic cleaner for encaustic floor tiles, wooden floors, slate and stone. Add 2–3 tablespoons of Basic Magic to a bucket and half-fill with hot water. Used in this way the solution will not leave a chalky film, so mop and leave to dry. This cleaner will cut through dirt and grease and, being non-acidic, will not harm natural materials.

I use this routinely on my tiled floors.

The magic of Pure Magic

My Pure Magic is absolutely true to its name. I am often asked how I came up with this simple, natural and amazing recipe. Now that we know and love it, many will remember the recipe off by heart and mix it quickly and effortlessly. Looking back, though, it wasn't simple at all and trying to get it just right certainly was a lesson in chemistry. I had to learn to understand a little bit about absorption rates, emulsifiers, pH balance, crystallisation, emulsification and natural acids – words that hadn't been part of my vocabulary until I decided to ditch harmful chemicals. Although it is a simple mix, believe me, it certainly gave me the run around.

I so wish I had paid more attention in chemistry lessons at school, though, as had they been a little more interesting and practical I am sure I would have been all ears.

I adore Pure Magic in its spray form, I consider it to be 'the best' toilet cleaner. Of all of my recipes this probably is the one that gave me the most excitement when it was developed.

Here are a couple of additions that expand the repertoire of our standard Pure Magic recipe.

Pure Magic gel

Pure Magic is a fine spray, and as such I found it wasn't easy to get into those hard-to-reach areas. I needed something thick and gloopy that would sit in place, tackling stains without running off. So here we have Pure Magic Gel – a gorgeous, thick, non-toxic Pure Magic that will stay where it is put! This is a sample recipe yielding around 200g (7oz) that can be scaled up if required. My bottle is quite small and I use this for tough jobs, choosing Pure Magic in its original form in my spray bottle for regular cleaning.

Xanthan gum is used to improve the crumb in gluten-free baked goods and is widely used in cosmetics; you can find it in the gluten-free section of the supermarket. Out-of-date (expired) xanthan gum is fine for this recipe.

You will need

500ml (17fl oz) heatproof jug
digital weighing scales
small whisk
upcycled shampoo bottle with a screwtop lid and squirt nozzle hole
small funnel (optional)

10ml (⅓fl oz) eco-friendly washing-up liquid
½ tsp xanthan gum
100g (3½oz) citric acid
75ml (2½fl oz) just-boiled water
1–2 drops of lemon essential oil (optional)

With the jug on the scales, weigh into it the washing-up liquid. Add the xanthan gum (the thickener) and stir with the small whisk to a thick paste.

Then add the citric acid and pour over the just-boiled water. Stir until the citric acid dissolves – at the same time the xanthan gum gets to work and thickens the mix. Leave to cool slightly, then stir in the essential oil, if using. Pour into the bottle, using the funnel as an aid.

The resultant thick yet squirtable (if that's a word) gel can be directed under the toilet rim, around the base of taps, around the plug hole and along stained grouting and will stay in place, thereby giving it a chance to dissolve stains and limescale without running off.

See the deep clean of a badly stained toilet on pages 51–54.

Pure Magic flush

Pure Magic is proven to be a fantastic toilet cleaner, with so many other uses that I have listed on pages 26–28. Many have asked whether the water and toilet cistern itself can be cleaned and keep clear of limescale build-up. Also, how to keep the hidden area under the rim clear of limescale and water marks. Try my Pure Magic Flush!

I remember those blocks that could be added to the toilet cistern to turn the flushing water blue or green – to then flush a whole concoction of harmful chemicals into the waterways. I used to use them all the time! I wanted some way to do this using my Pure Magic but in an eco-friendly way. I needed slow-release and came up with this simple idea.

When testing this recipe, the trials went on over several weeks. I started with a plastic bottle, filled it with water, then added several drops of blue food colouring. I needed to see how many flushes could be achieved before the water turned from blue to clear. I kept a gate chart outside the bathroom and the instructions were that anyone using the toilet, after washing their hands, had to add to the paper chart on the table just outside.

It took around 20 flushes before the water was clear again and the bottle in the cistern contained an amount of just-clear water where it had taken water back in through the hole. I stopped adding colouring to my mix, I continued using Pure Magic rather than coloured water and finally, after various experiments I was happy. My cistern on the inside was no longer an ugly yellow colour, was clear of a grey film on the unpolished rough clay and was now bright white, just like the toilet bowl. The metal parts on the flush mechanism looked shiny and bright once more, too.

You will know when the solution is used up, as the bubbles will have gone when flushing. Also, some washing-up liquids bubble more than others, so you may want to adjust the dosage accordingly.

As an aside, I remember one of my first 'live' Pure Magic Flush efforts – I overdosed on the washing-up liquid and after the first flush bubbles filled the toilet bowl. We had visitors for a meal at that time and one friend came back from the loo asking whether all was okay with the toilet. I said I was working on another recipe, so everyone had a good laugh at my expense.

I add a bottle of Pure Magic Flush to the cistern as a one-off treatment every six months or so, preferring to use my Pure Magic spray as my daily clean routine.

You will need

digital weighing scales
1 litre (34fl oz) heatproof jug
metal spoon

1 litre (34fl oz) upcycled plastic bottle with screwtop lid
metal skewer
funnel (optional)

500g (7oz) citric acid
300ml (10fl oz) just-boiled water
20ml (½fl oz) eco-friendly washing-up liquid
a few drops of essential oil (optional)
a few drops of food or soap colouring (optional)

Measure the citric acid into a heatproof jug, pour over the just-boiled water and stir using the metal spoon until the solution is completely clear and not a single particle remains. Leave to cool, then add the washing-up liquid – I use less than in the standard recipe, otherwise you will create excess bubbles when flushing. Then add essential oil, if using, and food or soap colouring if you want to see how well it works and when to make some more. Though, to be honest, I don't want colours in the loo – it feels wrong, dated and unnecessary.

Take the plastic bottle and, using a hot metal skewer (I heat mine on the gas hob) make a hole in the neck of the bottle – about ½cm (¼in) in diameter. As you look at the bottle, place the hole about 5–8cm (2–3in) down from the lid.

Add the funnel to the bottle, if using, then pour in the citric acid mix, which will fill the bottle but not high enough to come out of the hole.

Take the full bottle to the toilet, remove the lid to the cistern and stand the bottle inside.

When the loo is flushed you will see that Pure Magic Flush will dispense a dose into the water as the cistern empties and then re-fills, once the bottle is agitated. This will happen every time the toilet is used. Being plastic, the bottle will move and float around.

Pure Magic FAQs

Crystallization

If your Pure Magic crystallizes, remove the spray nozzle and lay it in a bowl of warm water so that any crystals inside will quickly dissolve. The bottle (minus the spray nozzle) containing the solidified Pure Magic can then be stood in a pan of cold water and heated gently on the hob until the crystals dissolve. Alternatively, if your bottle is microwave-safe, place it (with the spray nozzle removed) in the microwave and heat in 20-second bursts, examining after each blast of energy until you see that the solution inside has returned to liquid.

Spray attachments

I have had many messages from 'green cleaners' saying they go through so many spray attachments and wonder whether it is because they are of poor quality. I think not – this is probably due to putting pressure on and forcing the trigger if and when it feels stiff. Resist the temptation and drop it into warm water instead. After a 5-minute soak, depress the trigger under the water to flush and release the mechanism.

Unlike proprietary cleaning products, we don't use chemical surfactants to keep solutions free-flowing and we sometimes have to give a manual helping hand to help products spray efficiently. Try to get into the habit of quickly rinsing the nozzle under the tap after using it.

Shelf life

Pure Magic has a long shelf life – at least a year. I tend to make a double batch – pop one half into my spray bottle and the other half into a glass bottle with a screwtop lid to use in the laundry and for other problems. One such second bottle I found at the back of my shelf. I had made bottles of it during a filming session and couldn't remember even making it. I had to look it up – that had been a year ago. The bottle was still absolutely fine and as clear as the first day I made it.

Overspray stickiness

There have been a fair few cries for help from new keen Pure Magic users asking why it's leaving a sticky residue. Pure Magic is not a surface spray; if not rinsed well it will dry sticky (which is why it can clog your spray nozzle), so either rinse well after use on sinks, baths, etc., or use my all-purpose spray cleaner on page 10 for a daily 'spray and go' on surfaces and toilet seats. Any sticky residue after using Pure Magic can be removed by using a warm damp cloth.

Overspray stains

I have had many a question re 'overspray', i.e. the user has been having a great time spraying the toilet or the sink to then find the next day Pure Magic overspray has stained or left a sticky residue on and around nearby paintwork, walls or floor. Pure Magic, being an acidic cleaner, can be neutralized using a base or alkaline solution. A wipe with Basic Magic or my cream cleaner should remove the overspray. For larger areas such as floors, 2–3 tablespoons of washing soda dissolved in a bucket of hot water and mopped over will clean any white stains or sticky residue.

Dry grease stain remover: Terre de Sommières

I came across this amazing natural grease remover on my European road trip when I was examining the availability of natural cleaning products on the supermarket shelves across France, Spain, Belgium and The Netherlands. The French supermarkets were amazing – being host to various brands of green cleaning ingredients such as green bleach, citric acid, washing soda, vinegars, eco-friendly washing-up liquids and spray bottles, to name but a few. I was in heaven. Among their collection was a tub I had not seen before – Terre de Sommières (Fuller's earth) – similar in appearance to diatomaceous earth, though this naturally occurring powdered clay is an absorbent stain remover and, again, one I would recommend for emergency situations.

I picked up a jar after reading the *mode d'emploi* (instructions) on the reverse label. I am so pleased I learned to speak French 20 or so years ago, after thinking there was no point in even trying when I was at school.

This dry stain remover is brilliant. It is safe to use on textiles including silk, leather, suede and nubuck, wood, marble and stone. I already had my own stain-removal recipes, but there are other situations where the stain may be troublesome or very large. A whole bottle of oil spilt on a carpet, for example – where to even start? Grease splashes on suede shoes or boots? Grease on a waterproof garment where wetting the stain and laundering isn't an option?

When I think about the number of questions I've received from readers saying they have residual staining after using a proprietary grease-removal product and is there anything that can be done, whereas I have never had anyone say a stain remains after using natural Terre de Sommières.

I put it to the test on a sizeable drizzle of grease spilt from a roasting pan as I took it from the oven. I had a huge ugly stain on the carpet, probably measuring a foot in length. I remembered my tub of Terre and sprinkled the fine light-brown powder over the stain. I massaged it in using a finger then left it. The next day I vacuumed the carpet, nearly forgetting I had treated the stain because the carpet is almost the same colour as the Terre. The stain had gone. Nothing remained. I recommend buying a small tub online to have in cases of emergency – a grease stain on a silk tie comes to mind!

Sticky stuff paste

This simple recipe is very effective and replaces the often-pricey shop-bought chemical solvents that promise to do the same job. I have had many a tip from followers suggesting I use lemon essential oil, but again – for the reasons I explain on page 182 – I continue to wean myself off them. I recall people having removed sticky residue on floors left by double-sided tape, and sticky residue from labels on new windows and window frames using this paste.

You will need

glass jar with a screwtop lid
pastry brush or spatula

50g (2oz) bicarbonate of soda
50ml (2fl oz) vegetable oil (or the cheapest oil you have)

Simply mix the bicarb and oil together in a jar. Obviously for a big job, scale up the recipe. Use an old pastry brush or spatula to apply the paste to the sticky label, label residue or sticky substance. Leave for a minimum of 15 minutes, then wipe or scrape off using a spatula.

Don't use on sticky labels on clothing as the oil will create another stain on the fabric – use my cream cleaner (see page 11) instead.

Dry cleaning foam

I regularly use this recipe around the home for the dry-ish cleaning of pillows, mattresses, quilts and stubborn carpet and upholstery stains. It uses just suds so it tends to be a safer, quicker and more effective option than over-wetting an item by using too much water; the item may suffer water damage, will definitely take forever to dry, can leave water marks and, in the case of carpets, cause shrinkage.

My dry-ish clean, with the option to add green bleach for severe stains, is very effective. I used to suggest using a plastic shower puff to both agitate the solution and produce the suds, then to apply and work at the item being cleaned. But as the shower puff is plastic – and if you don't already have one then you certainly shouldn't purchase a new one – try instead a loofah scourer to agitate the suds and a tea towel with a small pan lid to work at the stains.

Wrap an old cotton tea towel around the pan lid, hold onto the cloth and the lid handle and rub the flat, round surface on the material to clean – it is a fantastic tool on flat surfaces and larger areas. Have you ever witnessed those industrial-sized floor-cleaning machines using two large circular pads? That's where I got my inspiration. Try dipping the cloth-covered pan lid into the suds, then work it in a circular motion on mattresses, carpets, upholstery, etc. Use a second dry cloth to then wipe over the area that has been cleaned to dry off as much surface moisture as possible. Using a pan lid helps the process because less energy is needed, so a larger area can be cleaned in one go.

You will need

- large bowl
- wooden spoon
- natural loofah scourer
- 2 old cotton tea towels
- small domed pan lid with handle (mine is glass with a metal rim and handle) 15–20cm (6–8in) in diameter

- 4 tbsp washing soda
- 2 tsp green bleach (see note below)
- 100ml (3½fl oz) just-boiled water
- 150ml (5½fl oz) cold water
- 20ml (¾fl oz) eco-friendly washing-up liquid
- sugar shaker filled with bicarbonate of soda for tougher areas

Add the washing soda and green bleach to the bowl, pour over the just-boiled water and stir with a spoon until dissolved and beginning to foam. Then add the cold water and washing-up liquid. Use the natural loofah to work at the mix until the bowl is filled with suds.

Wrap one of the tea towels around the pan lid and secure with your hand, then, holding the handle and cloth, dip the pan lid into the pillow of suds and start working at the stained area. Choosing a pan lid with a metal rim makes light work of the cleaning as the hard edge really helps to work the foam into the stains. Regularly move the cloth around the pan lid, as it will quickly lift the dirt. Any tough sections may benefit from a sprinkle of bicarbonate of soda from the sugar shaker. Once an area has been cleaned, wipe it over with the clean dry towel.

Again, always test a small area before diving in, especially on 100 per cent wool carpets and rugs. Depending on the type of stain (particularly urine), adding extra bicarbonate of soda can affect the carpet dye. Note: Include green bleach only when cleaning heavy stains on paler items – it is not recommended for black or dark upholstery or carpets.

For a safe spot-cleaning solution on urine, vomit, poo

- 2 tbsp white vinegar
- 1 tbsp eco-friendly washing-up liquid
- 250ml (9fl oz) tepid water

Combine all the ingredients for the solution, then use it to dab at the stain. Once the stain has been removed the whole area can be cleaned using the recipe and method above.

Dry cleaning foam FAQ

I used the dry cleaning foam on my dark-coloured upholstery and was left with white patches. What can I do?

Refrain from using the green bleach in the solution and don't overdo the extra bicarb when cleaning dark-coloured upholstery, as it can dry leaving a white, powdery, unsightly stain.

Brush the dry upholstery to remove any loose powder, then mix the vinegar spray below, which will neutralize the unsightly marks.

You will need

spray bottle
dry cloth

100ml (3½fl oz) white vinegar
100ml (3½fl oz) cold water

Combine the vinegar and water in a spray bottle, then spray the area and wipe over with the dry cloth to neutralize the effects of the bicarb. A whole seat or cushion should be sprayed to avoid water marks when dried.

Green bleach foam

This is a powerful mould buster for those difficult-to-treat places, including washing machine door seals, shower screen runners, badly stained and mouldy fridge seals and some silicone sealants.

I wanted a product that was non-acidic and therefore safe to use on the rubber seal of my washing machine, to kill and bleach out the mould and residual staining.

Mould build-up on a washing machine door seal is unsightly, can create odours and can shorten the life of the rubber. Acidic cleaners are not recommended on rubber because they can cause perishing, so a gentle, non-abrasive, non-acidic yet effective recipe was called for.

I had tried many things – very hot washes with green bleach, leaving washing soda and green bleach in the creases of the seal overnight before a hot wash the next day – but nothing was shifting the stubborn, unsightly, black staining.

I would just like to add a small note here, because as the washing machine was my first major clean when 'going green' and I have since taken great pride in the well-being of my machine, as a reader I would be asking, why now at this late stage is she writing about mould staining? Surely her machine is always sparkling and what must she be doing to create such a mould problem? I need to put the record straight.

The mould discovery was made when I returned from six weeks of working away. The house had continued to be lived in during my absence, but during the time I had been away my machine had suffered a terrific mould and stain problem. My assumptions were that it was partly because the machine had been used to wash very soiled clothing without first pre-soaking, and because the door and detergent dispenser had been closed when not in use.

Both of these things I don't do, choosing always to pre-soak very soiled working clothes, sports kits, etc., and secondly, when not in use I always leave the detergent dispenser and drum door open to allow air to circulate and any moisture to evaporate, which if left will cause mould. Although I was saddened and had to live with the mould for many weeks until I fathomed a remedy, as an outcome I am very pleased because a new, very effective recipe was the result.

Just as I needed Pure Magic Gel as a product to stay where I wanted it to (though not for the washing machine, due to its acidity), the same applied to Green Bleach Foam. I needed something that could be painted onto that stained rubber and left in place to do its work.

Enter green bleach foam!

For those not familiar with green bleach (my nickname for sodium percarbonate), here is a quick explanation. Green bleach takes the form of very small white granules, and a teaspoon here or there is all that is needed to do a huge job! It is used on its own to whiten and brighten laundry and as a stain remover in the recipe that follows, as well as many other recipes in this book.

It is SO good, and those that have made the switch and have 'gone green' will join me as I applaud it. Thanks to green bleach and Pure Magic (not used together), my previous reliance on harmful chlorine bleach, biological detergents and chemical-heavy cleaning products is now a thing of the past.

Compared to other natural cleaning ingredients, green bleach is expensive, so I use it sparingly and only when necessary. Those that have been using it and understand it will know that once activated it will only remain effective for 6 or 7 hours, so it is not something that can be added to any of my shelf-stable recipes.

You will need

500ml (17fl oz) measuring jug
small whisk
old pastry brush

½ tsp xanthan gum (perfect use for out-of-date xanthan gum)
1 tbsp vegetable glycerine
4 tsp green bleach (sodium percarbonate)
150ml (5½fl oz) just-boiled water

For the wash cycle

2 tbsp washing soda
4 tsp green bleach

Add the xanthan gum into the jug, then add the vegetable glycerine and stir to form a thick paste. It is necessary to do this first, otherwise the xanthan gum doesn't mix smoothly and will sit in lumps. Add then the green bleach and stir into the paste. Pour over the just-boiled water and continue to stir until the mix thickens, foams and rises up the jug.

Take the jug of foam and place it into the drum of the machine. Use the pastry brush to apply the hot foam, brushing it between the folds of the rubber, up the sides, then pull out the front and brush into every nook and cranny. The drum can catch any spills or drips. Use up all of the foam by filling the rubber crease to the brim.

Leave the foam in place for 6 or 7 hours or overnight, which is the maximum length of time that green bleach will last once activated, then return to the machine. Add 2 tablespoons of washing soda and 4 teaspoons of green bleach into the drum (it doesn't matter that it drops through the holes in the drum), close the machine door and switch on a hot 90°C wash cycle – mine takes 2 hours.

The result? Mould staining will be gone, though for very stained rubbers a repeat session may be needed. Any residual staining that might remain on the wall of the rubber will be softened and can be easily wiped away using Basic Magic and a dry cloth (see page 46).

To prevent further issues of mould build-up, always leave the machine door and detergent dispenser open.

Shower base runners, rubber seals and silicone sealants

Green bleach foam can be used to clean stained shower base runners and rubber seals and silicone sealants around baths, etc. The foam will stay in place and allow the green bleach to do its work. I have had many people telling me this works a treat, though I haven't been able to put it to the test myself yet as I have a free-standing bath without the need for sealants.

Cleaning patios, slippery steps, tarmac, pavers and decking

Damp shady areas that rarely see sunshine will develop green algae and moss. After the winter's wear and tear, patios, sitting areas and stone steps will be weathered, grubby and, worst of all, slippery. Path and patio cleaning products are available, but they are expensive and may well contain a cocktail of chemicals that through seepage into the soil will find their way into our rivers and waterways. Unsightly areas can be cleaned up any time of the year but particularly in spring when the days are longer and outside spaces are used more frequently, but also Mother Nature is on hand to help with the cleaning.

I have a natural-stone step and acidic chemicals should not be used on stone, slate, granite or marble because the acid will etch and harm the surface. Following a winter of dog footprints, marks from garden pots, green algae and rotted leaf mould, my step looked forlorn.

Some may say, save time – use a power washer. I have three concerns about using the power washer on my step. One is the amount of energy it uses when I have my own available, the second is the excess water being used when it is free from the sky, and thirdly, power washers can remove the natural patina of stone and damage wooden surfaces, making them porous and weakening their structure.

I decided to clean my step and engage in a much-needed workout at the same time; once I had tired after applying the natural products, I knew I could hand over to Mother Nature, who would do the final clean, rinse and dry for me – for free and with no harm to the environment. As with any natural treatment that you've not tried before, test a small area first to be sure you are happy with the result and there is no damage.

For best results, choose a time when thundery showers are in the weather forecast. Spring cleaning at its best!

You will need

- long-handled stiff yard brush
- watering can of rainwater (or tap water if you don't have a water butt)
- washing soda (sodium carbonate – in a flour shaker or a large glass jar with a screwtop metal lid that has large holes drilled into it)
- unperfumed eco-friendly washing-up liquid (no citrus scents that will create a fizz and weaken the cleaning effectiveness)

Wait for the sky to be leaden as a sign that heavy rain is coming soon. Using the watering can of rainwater (or tap water) wet the area to be cleaned – in my case my natural stone large step. Then sprinkle washing soda liberally over the green algae, moss, slippery wooden surface or grubby patio.

Drizzle over washing-up liquid and, using the yard brush, work the two ingredients together – the moisture already on the step, the washing soda and washing-up liquid will come together to make a thick, creamy solution that you can work into the stains.

This bit of effort is no real hardship, as proprietary toxic chemical cleaners will often instruct the user to brush in well.

Deciding to clean any outside space is always a good workout, so give that brush some action, paying extra attention to the badly stained areas, then leave it as it is. No need for any rinsing, for extra valuable tap water or, even worse, the power washer. The rest of the cleaning can be left to Mother Nature.

When the rain comes the cleaning will continue – Mother Nature will gently wash, then she'll rinse and when the sun comes out she will complete the task by further brightening and finally drying. My stone step had never looked so good.

This cleaning method has been used extensively by others and has successfully cleared moss from tarmac, stains on block paving, porcelain tiles, concrete paths and slippery York stone.

A strong washing soda solution can harm plants, so be careful around your treasured blooms. It didn't harm my grass but if in any doubt, maybe try a test area first.

Black spot lichen

I have had countless messages and questions from followers about black spots on their stonework, pavers and paths. They have tried natural products to no avail.

The black spots are probably black lichen and there are products on the market that promise to remove them. Often referred to as black spot remover, these products are very toxic and emblazoned with our well-recognized statement 'toxic to aquatic life with long-lasting effects' on the reverse label. Additional hazards are that they can give off toxic gas and cause severe burns and eye damage. One product I saw suggested wearing breathing apparatus while using it!

I spent two years trying different treatments and giving them time to see whether they worked. The best results came from diluted Pure Magic and full sunshine, and while it seems to have prevented the lichen spreading on the small section of York stone that I treated, it didn't remove it completely.

Green bleach sprinkled onto damp areas covered in black lichen made no difference whatsoever. So I have decided to live with my black lichen – the spores are in the air and it would be an uphill battle and a complete contradiction for me to use toxic chemicals repeatedly to keep my paths lichen-free. I now consider it to be part of the patina and natural ageing of my stone and paved areas.

I read somewhere that black lichen will absorb air pollutants – I have no idea whether that is true, though it does help me to not dislike it so much.

Cleaning a stone bird bath

I try to think about augmenting my recipes and making them work better or go further. Once the reader understands the use of acidic ingredients and alkaline ingredients, the simple rules, then with confidence it becomes easy and very satisfying to get better results.

Basic Magic (see page 43) can be mixed with green bleach safely to give an extra boost to heavy stains. I cleaned a very badly stained and water-marked stone bird bath using 3 tablespoons of Basic Magic and 1 teaspoon of green bleach swirled around with warm water. I left it to soak a couple of hours or so to reveal, once rinsed with clean clear rainwater, a beautifully clean bath for my wild birds.

Choose a sunny day, and once the algae and water stains have been cleaned, allow the sun to completely dry the stone, thereby destroying any residual algae. I had a little read around algae to discover it uses sunlight to produce energy, but too much can be damaging to them, which leads to increased cell death. They have limited protection against ultraviolet radiation.

TIP: A copper coin placed in the clean water will help prevent and slow down the growth of algae, but it doesn't stop it altogether. In the past, coins were made from 100 per cent copper, however, modern coins dating from 1982 are made from copper-plated zinc. I use three small half-inch pieces of copper piping, squashed flat, and they do a sterling job of keeping the water clear for longer.

Clearing green algae and mould spots

I get so many questions about this, especially in late spring and early summer, when we take out the garden furniture, seats and cushions along with the sun parasol. I have had requests from people wanting to clean up the green algae-covered fenders and weather shields on their boats. I know of people who have used Pure Magic to clean very badly stained UPVC, greenhouse glass and even gutters and green walls.

I have received some great before and after shots of sun parasols, green and mouldy because they suffered over the winter months, which once opened up, cleaned and offered up to the sun became bright and white once more.

You will need

old sink brush and cloths
sunshine

hot soapy water
Pure Magic (see page 7)

Wet the area to be cleaned with hot soapy water, then spray on Pure Magic and, using the old sink brush, work at the algae, mould spots and general grime. Pure Magic will kill mould spores, and if you choose a sunny day Mother Nature will assist in the stain removal. Rinse or wipe down well after use because it will dry sticky.

Note: If there are very large areas to clean or you prefer a non-acidic solution, Basic Magic (see page 43) will do the job and is more economical, but it isn't quite the beast that Pure Magic is.

Removing rust marks

Rust can create stubborn stains on so many items – on carpets from the rusted runners of old furniture, on fabrics from rusted buttons or zips, on shelves from rusted bases of cans and containers, and also outside on patios from rusted metal furniture, garden tools and, in my case, on my stone yard from rusted scaffolding posts.

Rust on stone

My house had a section of guttering replaced and scaffolding was erected to enable access to the area. The posts were in place for a number of weeks, as the work took longer than expected because it never seemed to stop raining.

Eventually, the gutters were fixed, the scaffolding removed and all was back to normal – apart from an ugly, large, 15–20cm (6–8-inch) square of rust on my York stone yard. Every time I went outside I looked at it – I had to try to sort the rust stain. Pure Magic to the rescue.

You will need

> old sink brush
> watering can of clean water
>
> water spray
> Pure Magic (see page 7)
> table salt

If the stone is dry, spray with water to dampen the stain. Then spray Pure Magic and add a sprinkle of table salt. Using an old sink brush, work the ingredients into the stain using circular motions. The solution will create a foam, and once it does, leave it to soak.

After a few hours, rinse with clean water and the rust stain will have dissolved. My stain was very bad and needed a second application.

Acidic cleaners on natural stone are not recommended for repeated use, so a thorough rinse using clean water is essential. My York stone was not damaged following this 'one-off' treatment.

Rust on paintwork, in sinks and on shelves

Spray Pure Magic over the stain and leave to soak for up to half an hour – a sprinkle of salt can help here, scrubbed in to act as an abrasive. Using a damp cloth, rub at the stain and you will see the unsightly rust marks left from cans or other metal items quickly dissolve.

Rusted metal

Clean rust from metal outdoor furniture and rusted garden tools – I even cleaned up my rusted old bike – using Pure Magic, fine wire wool and a sprinkle of table salt to add a little abrasion. Pure Magic gel (see page 49) is also effective and will go further because it can be painted on and will not run off.

Rust on carpets

Rust stains on carpets left from a leaking radiator or maybe a rusted metal castor on the base of an old piece of furniture are unsightly but can be dealt with effectively.

You will need

wooden fork, spoon or old toothbrush
cloths

water spray
Pure Magic (see page 7)

Start by lightly wetting the rust spot using a spray of water, then add a spray of Pure Magic and massage in using either your fingers (though they will get sticky) or the back of a small wooden fork or spoon or a toothbrush.

Leave it to do its work – popping back from time to time, giving it another poke around with the wooden fork. You will see that the rust will begin to dissolve and a pale caramel foam will be produced.

Using a clean damp cloth and clean water, dab at the stain. The rust will have dissolved and the carpet below will be free of stain. As the mixture is sticky it is important to keep rinsing the cloth and dabbing at the damp patch to make sure the previously stained area is clear of product.

Neutralizing stains

I have had many cries for help over time from enthusiastic green cleaners who have gone to town when using Pure Magic, Basic Magic, washing soda, etc. Maybe a toilet has been successfully cleaned but then the next day there is evidence of overspray on the wall or floor, which has left white marks.

Similarly, I have others who have told me their Basic Magic has left a ring mark on wood or a dark stain on a work surface. Try to think about 'false friends' and the fact that acids and alkaline products do not work well together because they cancel each other out. We very rarely use lemon and bicarb together, for example, as the resulting fizz is a chemical reaction resulting in the two products cancelling each other out to leave simply an inert salt.

However, we can apply this chemical reaction to our advantage as a stain neutralizer. For example: a stain from Pure Magic (being acid) can be neutralized using a hot washing soda solution (alkaline). The hot water and washing soda will dissolve, neutralize and remove it. A stain left by washing soda (alkaline) on wood can be neutralized using a spray of vinegar or lemon juice (acid). Pure Magic is also acidic, but it can be too harsh to use in this situation – always try a small area first rather than diving in and potentially spreading the stain further.

Pumice stone tricks

Natural pumice stone – a type of volcanic rock that forms when lava suddenly cools during an eruption – is sponge-like in appearance, porous and lightweight. It's a great exfoliator for hard skin and in its ground form I have read that it is used as an abrasive ingredient in dentistry for polishing teeth.

I have discovered that it can add that extra cleaning boost when used with bicarbonate of soda or my cream cleaner (see page 11). I have a pumice stone that I save for cleaning – it is worn and smooth at one end so I can be sure it will not scratch any surface. There are square pumice stones that are machine cut, but if you are using these, I would recommend blunting the edges on a hard surface outside first (on concrete, for example) to prevent any scratching.

Oven glass doors

The pumice stone can help when cleaning stubborn splashes and burnt-on food on a glass oven door.

You will need

- worn, smooth-edged pumice stone soaked in warm water
- cloth

Oven Magic (see page 97), cream cleaner or a simple bicarb paste (bicarbonate of soda mixed with warm water)
small bowl of warm soapy water (washing-up liquid/dish soap and water)
small bowl of bicarbonate of soda

Apply a layer of the cleaning product you decide to use – Oven Magic, cream cleaner or bicarb paste – to cover the glass oven door. Take the already dampened pumice stone and using small circular movements, work at those stubborn, baked-on stains. I find the help from the pumice stone is more effective than fine wire wool.

Note: Don't use pumice stone on stainless steel or metal as it can scratch, and always use it pre-soaked and dipped in a product, not dry on its own.

Encaustic and terracotta tiles

I have a beautiful encaustic-tiled hall floor. However, at one end it had become very badly marked. A mix of scuffs, scratches and unsightly marks that had built up over years. I had tried everything – my floor cleaner, my cream cleaner and a dry cloth, and I had even resorted to Pure Magic and fine wire wool, knowing the latter attempt was harmful to the floor, being acidic, but still nothing budged them. Until I reached for my pumice stone.

You will need

worn, smooth-edged pumice stone
bucket of warm soapy water
cloths
sink brush

small bowl with a quantity of bicarbonate of soda –
   2–3 tbsp to start

Start by soaking the pumice stone in the bucket of warm soapy water. The pumice will float, but by soaking it the stone becomes softer.

Wet the marked floor area using the cloth dipped into warm soapy water and wrung out. Take the wet pumice stone and dip one end into the bicarbonate of soda. Work then in a small circular motion and see those aged scratches and marks disappear. Get into the routine of regularly dabbing into the bicarb so that the stone is not directly scouring the tiles.

The abrasion from the bicarb and pumice returned my very old floor to its former glory with no scratches and no need for severe acidic or harmful chemical cleaners.

While the floor was wet and splattered with bicarb I took the opportunity to clean up the grouting, too. An old sink brush dipped into the bucket of water quickly worked at the grouting. Little did I know the original grouting colour was grey and not black!

Finish by mopping over with clean warm soapy water and leave to dry.

Paint splashes, tile adhesive and concrete splashes

I have a slate-tiled outdoor step into the garage, which I took note of after giving the garage a good clear out one sunny summer day. For many years I had ignored the white paint splashes on the dark grey, but I also noticed a blob of concrete or maybe excess tile adhesive. Either way, all of it was stuck solid. Taking a wet pumice stone dipped in dry bicarb and some elbow grease, the paint, adhesive and concrete were smoothed away without scratching my much-loved slate. Rather than going out to purchase chemical-heavy paint, cement, grout and mortar remover, my little pumice stone and bicarb did the trick.

Suede

A metal-toothed brush specifically designed for suede shoes does a great job of gently lifting the fabric's pile, especially after cleaning. I had cleaned a pair of trainers for my granddaughter that had panels of suede material and strips of leather, and finding myself without a suede brush I discovered that a rub over with a dry pumice stone had the same effect, lifting the pile and leaving an even colour to the suede.

TIP: A clean white pencil rubber can also help to remove light scuffs from suede – always test an area first.

Toilet

Many 'green cleaners' have had such fantastic success using my Pure Magic solution, which has dissolved staining and limescale from sanitaryware. For those toilets left with a stubborn water mark just on the water level, try using this method.

You will need

toilet brush or old sponge and bucket
rubber gloves
small bowl of hot water
worn, smooth-edged pumice stone

1–2 tsp citric acid in a small cup or bowl

Push the water back up the U bend using a toilet brush, or decant some of the water using a sponge, gloved hands and a bucket, thereby exposing the ring of limescale staining.

If you don't have a toilet brush (I know some people hate them) and you don't fancy decanting the water by hand, another method is to pour a full bucket of water into the toilet in a swift action. The water will be pushed back in the same way, exposing the stained water line.

Take the small bowl of hot water and wet the pumice stone. Dip the warmed pumice into the citric acid, then using the crystal-coated pumice, rub away at the limescale water line. The action from the citric acid as it dissolves, plus the non-scratch abrasion from the pumice stone, will quickly dissolve that stubborn mark.

Wood burner glass

Glass doors can get heavily marked, and I have had many messages from people who have moved into a house with a badly marked stove glass, which has resisted my usual method of dipping damp newspaper into cold ash and rubbing it over the glass – a quick and easy daily routine that keeps the glass sparkling. When that hasn't worked, some have used a spray of Pure Magic (see page 7), while others prefer my cream cleaner (see page 11) and a dry cloth. However, if all of these have failed, try this.

You will need

- worn, smooth-edged pumice stone
- cloth

- small bowl of warm soapy water (eco-friendly washing-up liquid/dish soap and water)
- small bowl of bicarbonate of soda

Soak the pumice stone in the soapy water – the pumice doesn't get saturated and sink to the bottom of the bowl, it will continue to float. Dip one end of the wet pumice into the bowl of bicarbonate of soda and use it to then work at the glass.

Regularly dip the pumice back into the water and then into the bicarb, cleaning in a small, circular motion. Always make sure there is a good coating of bicarb on the stone. You will see that the glass cleans up a treat without scratching. Wipe over with a clean damp cloth.

NATURE'S FREEBIES: During the winter months I do two things daily: I eat an orange to top up my vitamin C levels and use my wood-burning stove for heat. I never discard the orange peelings; I leave them in a bowl or basket by the fire until they have dried completely and will readily snap between the fingers. Once dried they make the perfect fire starter, rather than having to resort to proprietary kerosene products. A handful of dried peel, a few sticks of kindling wood laid over, then I light the peels using a match and the fire is going and ready for logs once fully lit.

Bonus wood ash tips

I don't discard wood ash. This very fine, light-grey powder has many uses and I save mine in a dustbin (the old-fashioned galvanized bins of yesteryear) – no plastic bins, in case there is any residual heat in the embers. I use it then as follows.

Garden: The high-potash content of ash means it is ideal to use around most of my soft fruit bushes, including raspberries, currants and gooseberries. I mix it into any soil used to grow fruiting vegetables, especially tomatoes. It apparently improves hardiness, disease resistance and productivity. I have read that it can be used as an excellent substitute for commercial lime (which has a high carbon footprint) to reduce acidity in garden soils, because wood ash is high in calcium carbonate (lime). My soil welcomes a light top dressing of ash, usually in autumn. However, you should only use it if you need to; conduct a pH test to determine if your soil is acidic or too alkaline to add ash.

Slugs and snails: Deter slugs and snails using a sprinkling of wood ash – they will not venture over the fine dry powder. I tend to run out with a sugar shaker of wood ash after a thunderstorm when the weather is warm and humid and I know an army of slugs and snails will be out overnight to munch on my lettuce. A border of wood ash around my bed of lettuce will keep them safe until the next downpour.

Slippery paths: During winter time a sprinkle of wood ash over walking or driving areas will add traction to a slippery surface. There is a slight slope into my garage and one year, after a fall of snow, rain and then ice, trying to drive the car into the garage was impossible. The wheels were spinning and I thought the car would need to be left outside. Out with a few shovels of wood ash sprinkled over the icy driveway and the wheels were able to grip the surface and my car was back where I wanted it.

Tomatoes: I did a little experiment after reading that fine wood ash will preserve tomatoes. Could this be true? I took a small wooden box, spooned in cold wood ash to a depth of about 5cm (2in), then added 8 cherry tomatoes and covered them well with more wood ash, dated them and left them in the garage. The month was March. These were not home-grown tomatoes, they were bought from the supermarket, and not recently either, as they had been in the fridge over a week or so. I visited the box again in May to uncover my tomatoes. I was amazed – my 8-week-old tomatoes were only very slightly wrinkled and after a wash were still firm and juicy inside. A further soak in ice-cold water and those wrinkly skins recovered. This will be one to try when my home-grown tomatoes are coming to the end of their season. Could I save fresh home-grown tomatoes for Christmas?

Marks on wood

Many questions arise about how to eliminate marks on wood, and these can take various forms: cup rings, water marks, black stains from plant pots, grease, various spills and even scorches. Obviously, there are many problems here and not one method will fix all, so I often find myself asking people to follow a checklist. However, first and foremost, for the expensive, quality French-polished items I would call in the professionals.

Cup rings, water marks and more

For cup rings, unknown stains and water marks, a warm, damp cloth dipped in dry bicarbonate of soda can sometimes remove a stain, especially if it is recent. Massage the mix into the wood then wipe away using a clean, rinsed-out cloth.

Scratches and some stains can be covered using a walnut, broken in half, rubbing the fleshy raw edge along the offending scratch or stain.

If staining persists after using the bicarb, I reach for my steam iron. I have used this on cup rings, water marks and a very black stain left from a plant pot. With this method, please proceed with caution, start slowly, don't rush and don't try it if the furniture is very precious. I used this successfully on a 'budget buy' nest of tables and on my untreated wooden kitchen table (it had a black stain from the plant pot), but you will have to decide whether this one is for you and your furniture.

I recall one cry for help from someone who, after removing the tablecloth following a large family meal, found a heat ring at each place setting because neither place mats nor a table protector had been used. The decision was made that she would have a go herself using the steam method, and if it was to fail then the table would have to be repolished anyway. To her delight, taking each heat ring very slowly and carefully, she returned the table to its former glory.

You will need

clean, thick tea towel, or a thinner piece of cotton
   folded to double thickness
steam iron

Use caution and take your time. Turn the iron onto the steam setting and medium heat. Lay the towel over the stain and very gently offer the steam from the iron over the towel – holding it above it, not touching it or applying any pressure.

Remove the towel, have a look underneath, and if all is well try again, only this time lightly put pressure onto the towel using the plate of the iron for a few seconds only. Remove the towel, check, and if all is well, repeat – only this time iron onto the cloth laid over the mark.

Remove the iron and the towel again and check – you should see the marks are slowly fading away. Repeat as necessary until the mark has been removed.

When I cleaned the very black plant pot mark, at first I thought I had made it worse. The stain looked as though it had spread, was still black and looked very wet. However, the stain disappeared once the table had dried – a wipe over using a dry cloth sprayed with my general polish (see page 15) and no one would ever know.

Grease stains on wood

For small grease stains, use my cream cleaner massaged in using a dry cloth. For very large grease or oil spills, a tub of Terre de Sommières (see page 56) will quickly absorb the spill and won't leave a trace.

Burns and scorches on wood

I don't have natural wooden kitchen work surfaces, though I have had many questions about scorch marks left by hot pans and/or utensils. Before going to the effort and/or expense of having these wooden surfaces sanded down to remove scorches or burn marks, try my cream cleaner followed by green bleach.

You will need

cloth
small cup or bowl
artist's paintbrush

cream cleaner (see page 11)
1 tsp green bleach
2–3 tbsp just-boiled water

Using a dry cloth dipped into a little cream cleaner, rub over the scorch mark in the direction of the wood grain. This can often lessen the mark. Then mix the green bleach with the just-boiled water in a small cup or bowl, stir until the bleach has completely dissolved, then use an artist's paintbrush to paint this mixture over the mark a little at a time.

Leave the mixture in place, and little by little the scorch should pale out. Depending on the severity of the scorch, repeat applications may be necessary – but allow the wood to dry between treatments.

> **TIP:** I have used green bleach to fade scorch marks on coloured fabrics. I scorched a green gingham tray cloth, which left a nasty brown mark. Green bleach took out the stain; it took several soaks but I was pleased that there was no alteration to the colours of the fabric.

DEEP CLEANS, BLOCKAGES AND REFRESHES

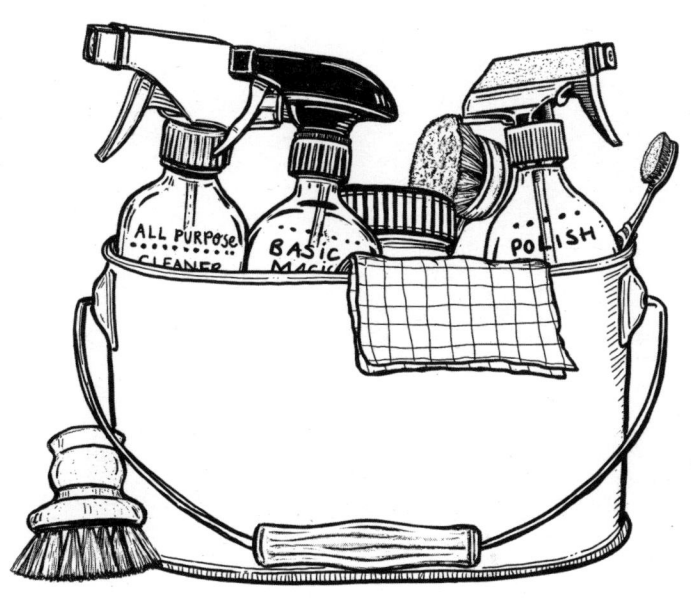

I enjoy a clean home, but I refuse to be a slave to it. I often wonder how some of the modern houses shown both on TV and social media manage to maintain their pale cream carpets, white walls and clean vases of freshly cut flowers on pristine furniture, especially when they show young children playing and pets running around. Impossible!

In a perfect, well-organized house, much more efficient than mine, prevention is the best cure and deep cleans may not be necessary. However, I have talked to too many young people who get stressed because their children make a mess, the dog walks mud on the carpet or the husband drips tea on the kitchen surfaces. This is actually normal home life (remember, your house should be a home, not a highly polished trophy), but we all have occasions when a deep, thorough clean becomes necessary. My first thoughts are taken to the aftermath of Christmas when, if you have been the host, the oven will have done its fair share of extra hours. Come to think of it, so has the dishwasher, and if you have had extra guests staying, probably the washing machine, bathroom, shower and toilet too! This chapter is all about getting your home back to normal after either a long time between deep cleans or once it has been put through its paces with visitors and heavy use.

Oven Magic

For me, moving away from toxic harmful chemicals for oven cleaning has been a triumph. When I think back to the awful products that I used to buy, which insisted on the wearing of protective gloves, the need for the room to be well ventilated and plastic bags for soaking shelves that had to be disposed of carefully, you realize that we were, after all, working with hazardous chemicals. I remember when I once used an old pastry brush to apply the toxic caustic gel, only to find that within a matter of minutes the bristles on the brush had dissolved!

Fast-forward a number of years and I now have at my disposal a number of natural ingredients, simple methods and recipes that make oven cleaning a dream. I did, however, have a problem concerning my Aga, and as a result I have rehashed and improved my oven-cleaning regime. During the summer months I use my electric oven rather than the Aga, and I clean it with washing soda soaks for the shelf runners, grill pan and oven shelves.

> **NATURE'S FREEBIE:** My oven shelves are rarely badly stained, because at the first signs of baked-on foods they are routinely thrown out onto the lawn overnight. A quick wipe the next day and they are as clean as a whistle.

My Aga serves me well during the winter. She is expensive to run but at the same time she is a workhorse. She dries the laundry, warms the kitchen, can do certain ironing, will do her fair bit of stain-removal laundry overnight and, of course, cooks all of the meals and does the baking very cleverly without producing lingering kitchen smells.

In mid to late spring, in order to save energy, I turn the Aga off, at which point I can then give my girl her annual full clean. For those unfamiliar with an Aga, the oven is cast-iron and has to be left on all of the time to store heat and maintain temperature, so deep, thorough cleaning is not really possible until the oven is off and cold. While it is on and always hot, the enamel surface gets a wipe with a damp cloth and I manage to keep my lids free of baked-on splashes by always wiping them down with a damp cloth before closing them.

The 'big' clean is not as onerous as one would think, as any oven spills and splashes are baked off within the oven housing. Any oven spills that burn onto the oven racks are not allowed to build up and establish themselves, as it is no effort to take them outside after the evening meal, lay them out on the fresh grass, whatever the weather, then the next morning I can wipe them down using a cloth and they are clean and shiny and can go back into the oven. Mother Nature keeps on top of the shelves for me.

My problem area is the oven door, which is made from coated enamel on the outside, metal on the inside and packed with fibreglass insulation in between. This door can't be soaked in a hot washing soda solution, and I know that from experience. I tried one year to submerge only the stained surface to hopefully soak off the stains – not the whole door. I laid the stained side of the oven door down in just 1cm (½in) of washing soda solution, only to find the next day that the solution had seeped through the screw holes, into the fibreglass and rendered the door insulation useless. New inside cover, insulation and avoidable expense later, I now had to be very careful. I needed an oven- and Aga-friendly magic solution to my problem. I had to develop a recipe that would stay in place, not over-wet my appliance, and that would be non-acidic and able to dissolve away the unsightly burnt-on splashes on my oven door without scouring. My new Oven Magic recipe is terrific – Basic Magic in gloop form!

You will need

500ml (17fl oz) heatproof measuring jug
small whisk
old towel
old pastry brush
plastic fish slice or spatula
used flour or sugar bag

1 tsp xanthan gum
20ml (¾fl oz) unperfumed eco-friendly washing-up liquid
50g (2oz) washing soda
200ml (7fl oz) just-boiled water

Measure the xanthan gum into the measuring jug, add the washing-up liquid and whisk to a thick paste. Add the washing soda, stir, then add the just-boiled water. Keep stirring until the mix becomes very thick and gloopy.

When cleaning my Aga oven door, I lift the cooling door from its hinges and lay it upside down on an old towel to protect the work surface and to save the shiny enamel from getting scratched. With the inside of the grubby door facing upwards, still just slightly warm, having been switched off several hours before, I use the brush to apply the Oven Magic all over the stains. I apply a thick layer of gloop – about 1cm (½in) thick in places! This is great because it stays wherever I put it, no drips running down the sides of the door. I also brushed the (once-shiny) stainless-steel frames inside the oven housing, which were badly splattered.

I leave the gloop to work its magic, returning periodically to check on its progress, using the brush to swirl the gloop around to try to look underneath. You will see the Oven Magic turning from a translucent white colour to caramel and will realize that without any doubt this recipe is doing its work fantastically.

After 2 hours or so – though you can check yourself depending on how things were at the outset – I use a flexible spatula to scrape the Oven Magic from the oven door and into a used paper flour bag. This way it can be disposed of amongst the general refuse rather than poured down the sink. A wipe with warm soapy water and my Aga oven door and housing is so beautifully clean without any need for scrubbing or scraping. This recipe is a winner!

My Aga is over 26 years old and looks as clean as the day she came into my life. She is my friend and I love to welcome her back when the autumn returns, the nights get cold and I need a cosy friend to come home to with something tasty ticking away for many hours in the bottom oven.

The big oven clean-up

I clean both of my ovens once a year; the Aga in the spring when it is turned off to save energy, and the electric oven at the end of the summer before the Aga goes back on. For a lot of my life I had one electric oven, and though I didn't have a strict cleaning regime, I believe it should receive a thorough clean twice a year so that the job doesn't become onerous and hard work.

Oven cleaning is one of those jobs that can be creatively avoided because something else can always grab your attention, leaving the oven to be dealt with on another day. Trouble is, the longer it is left, the worse it gets. Once cleaned and gleaming I want to keep admiring it, satisfied that cleaning it wasn't so bad after all.

With this new recipe under my belt I felt I needed to include 'new and improved' instructions for cleaning both Aga and electric ovens. To test it even further, my family members enjoyed a free oven clean as I tried my new recipe and method on their ovens, oven doors, shelves and racks! I timed myself, too – two ovens (one standard oven and one multi oven – a microwave and oven combined) took me just over two hours.

Oven cleaning without the toxic chemicals is documented in my first book, *Clean & Green*, and I know so many people have been pleasantly surprised by its simplicity. Very greasy and grimy ovens can require some extra effort and 'elbow grease', but my new Oven Magic will reduce that work.

My original recipe used a simple bicarb and water paste, thickened slightly with xanthan gum, but Oven Magic is more powerful (being made from grease-busting washing soda) and therefore less elbow grease is required. I also prefer using a natural pumice stone rather than fine wire wool for difficult, stubborn areas. Pumice, unlike wire wool, will not shred fine metal particles that if not checked will turn rusty in the sink, resulting in another clean-up job.

NOTE: Washing soda and Oven Magic are not to be used on aluminium parts, as it may permanently tarnish the metal. Do not apply the Oven Magic to non-stick oven coatings that usually have a matt grey, rough finish. These are often found on the sides and back of an oven and shouldn't need cleaning.

I have divided oven cleaning into two operations. One is a soak of removable parts – that is, shelves, racks, trays and runners. The second operation is the full oven – the cleaning of the oven carcass and door.

For the soak

You will need

hot water
sink or plastic box large enough to hold the shelves and runners (I have some followers who use a wheelbarrow!)

6–8 tbsp washing soda

Remove the metal shelves, side runners and drip tray – in fact, all removable items, and soak them in a hot washing soda solution.

In the sink, box or wheelbarrow, add the washing soda and the shelves and runners and pour over sufficient very hot water to cover the items. Leave to soak for at least 1 hour, but several hours or overnight is better. I have found that if the items are hand hot (rather than cold) when submerged, the cleaning is quicker and more effective, but you may want to avoid shelves becoming too hot if you are using a plastic box or plastic wheelbarrow.

After the soak, lift your shelves out of the brown murky water and wipe clean – that's it. You can pour the water down the drain knowing no harm is being done.

TIP: Clean stained lidded casserole dishes and pans in the Aga while you sleep. Add a tablespoon of washing soda and a teaspoon of green bleach to your stained cooking pot. Fill to almost the top with cold water, on with the lid and into the simmering (low) oven overnight. Next day, pour away the solution, wipe and your pan is returned to its former glory.

For a full oven clean

You will need

large roasting tin
worn, smooth-edged pumice stone
1 litre (34fl oz) heatproof jug or bowl
whisk
old towel
rubber gloves (optional)
old pastry brush
bench scraper or plastic spatula
used flour or sugar bag

60ml (2fl oz) unperfumed eco-friendly washing-up liquid
3 tsp xanthan gum
150g (5½oz) washing soda
600ml (1 pint) just-boiled water
bicarbonate of soda

Start by boiling a kettle of water. Place the large roasting tin on the floor of the empty oven housing. Switch on the oven to 100°C (212°F). Once the oven has reached temperature, open the door and pour a full kettle of boiling water into the roasting tin. Close the oven door, switch off the oven and leave for 20 minutes. The heat and the steam will soften the baked-on food splashes that are covering your oven sides and door. You can, of course, skip this step if your oven has a steam setting designed specifically for this purpose.

During this time you can make up your Oven Magic. Soak your pumice stone in a bowl of hot water and get ready to go! Place the washing-up liquid and xanthan gum into the heatproof jug or bowl and stir together to a paste. Stir in the washing soda then add the just-boiled water, a little at a time, until it becomes a thick gloopy mix.

When the 20 minutes is up, return to the oven. You will see that the glass door has steamed up and the oven sides are moist. Remove the roasting tin and carefully pour the hot water into a bowl with washing-up liquid – you can reuse it for any washing up later.

To make your oven easier to work on, unhinge the door if you can (your oven handbook should give instructions) and place it on an old towel on a work surface to clean. Reaching the back of the oven housing is then easier too. Many modern ovens allow the oven door to glide under the oven for easier access.

On with rubber gloves (if you choose to wear them) and start to brush on the Oven Magic. Put plenty on – brushing the sides, floor and door of the oven. Leave for at least 30 minutes, or for a very stained oven I would close the door (if still in situ) and leave for an hour or more before checking and carrying out a test. Periodically, use the pastry brush in circular motions to check whether the burnt-on debris is lifting and changing the Oven Magic gloop from white to a pale caramel. If this is the case, take the spatula and swipe across the side or door to check that food splashes, grease and staining have dissolved.

If you see any stubborn splashes or burnt-on marks left behind, use the wet pumice stone, dipped in Oven Magic, to rub at the area. The marks will easily lift without scratching the metal or glass of the oven door.

When, after a number of checks, you are happy that the oven sides, floor and door are clean, it is time for the big reveal. Remove the gloop using the flexible spatula and transfer into a used empty flour or sugar bag and pop into the refuse. After wiping away the oven magic, any stubborn remaining burnt-on areas that were missed can be quickly removed using a wet, smooth pumice stone dipped in dry bicarbonate of soda. The oven housing and door glass will not scratch if the pumice is wet.

Use a bowl of hot soapy water to finish the clean and remove any Oven Magic residue.

Your oven is sparkling – no fumes, no harmful chemicals, no wire wool scrubbing and minimal cost.

Once clean it is quite easy to keep the oven looking good for many months if you get into the habit of doing the following: every time you use the oven, wipe the inside of the glass door

while still warm (not scorching hot) with a clean, damp cloth. You will be surprised – just baking a loaf of bread, which you may consider a clean use of the oven, can leave a brown film on the glass door. Fat splashes will just wipe off if cleaned every time the oven is used. Just don't allow repeated use of the oven to bake them solid.

Aluminium oven filters

Many followers request help with cleaning aluminium filters housed in stainless-steel cooker hoods. These filters obviously work hard at sucking food smells, steam, fats and moisture from the kitchen during cooking, so it is no surprise that they will become discoloured, greasy and unsightly.

Washing soda, though a fantastic grease buster, should not be used on aluminium. I would also refrain from popping them into the dishwasher, because most dishwasher detergents will contain sodium carbonate (washing soda). We have green bleach, however, which will do a sterling job.

You will need

sink or container large enough to lie the filters in

2–3 tsp green bleach (sodium percarbonate)
just-boiled water

Simply place the filters in the sink or container, sprinkle over the green bleach and pour over a kettle of just-boiled water and leave to soak.

As eco-friendly green bleach once activated will only live around 6 or 7 hours – after which time it decomposes into soda ash, oxygen and water – a soak beyond this time is not going to do any more work. So remove the filters and pour the stained water down the sink. Wash clean in warm soapy water, air dry and your cooker filters are effortlessly clean without permanently staining the aluminium.

The stinky sink

I love my clean kitchen sink. It is spruced up daily using either my cream cleaner (see page 11), my all-purpose spray cleaner (see page 10), Basic Magic (see page 43), green bleach or Pure Magic (see page 7), whichever is to hand that morning. I regularly use a washing soda solution to degrease and deodorize. However, one time I walked into the kitchen and detected a pong coming from the sink. How could this be? It was clean, white, shiny, and the drain outside was clear. What was going on?

What was to be revealed was a chamber of horrors I never knew was lurking right under my own nose . . .

My sink has a plug hole with a central, large, ridged screw, and the plug cover is exactly the right size to fit the ridges and is designed to be used as the screwdriver, though I didn't know this at the time, so I used an old dessert spoon to remove it instead. If you do this and have never done it before I would recommend investing in a replacement rubber seal. Sink rubber seals are readily available in hardware stores and are not expensive. Having gone to the trouble of removing the plug cover, it is worth replacing the seal, and in some cases the seal may have started to perish and will have been held in place and continued to provide waterproofing simply by the amount of gunk surrounding it.

You will need

bucket
replacement seal
plug cover, old dessert spoon or screwdriver, if you
    have one
used paper flour or sugar bag
kitchen paper

bowl of hot soapy water
Basic Magic (page 43)
1 tsp green bleach

Make sure the space in the cupboard under the sink is empty and slide in a bucket to catch the drips. Have a bowl of hot soapy water to hand, because you will not be able to use the sink while you are cleaning it.

Using the outer edge of the metal sink plug cover, dessert spoon or a screwdriver specifically for the job, remove the screw in the centre of the plug hole by turning it anti-clockwise. Mine was terribly stiff, but slowly the large screw came up – black, very unsightly and smelly. Drop that straight into the bowl of hot soapy water.

When I carefully lifted the plug cover it revealed a stinky, slimy, thick black mass – I couldn't believe it. Here was lurking many years of food sludge. After a sit down to recover and decide what to do next, I used the old spoon to scrape out several tablespoons of sludge and placed them into a used paper sugar bag to chuck in the bin rather than trying to wash it down the sink.

I then used dry kitchen paper to wipe out the layer of residue remaining. The seal itself was intact, hadn't stretched or perished though I did have a spare just in case.

Wash all of the mucky items in the bowl of water – refrain from using the sink at all because, of course, any water would run straight into the bucket, though a few drips here and there were inevitable. I used a spray of Basic Magic, being non-acidic, to finish the clean, and then I sprinkled 1 teaspoon of green bleach down the pipe.

Once all was clean, I renewed the seal, laying it around the sink hole. I then added the metal plug hole cover. This is where you need two hands; I removed the bucket and with one hand (my left hand as I am right-handed), I put the pipe under the sink back up to its original position and with my right hand I was able to return the clean screw to the centre of the plug hole cover. Turning the screw clockwise by hand connected it to the pipe being held in place by my left hand.

Continue to turn the screw by hand until it feels secure, then fully tighten using the metal plug cover, spoon or screwdriver.

Run fresh water into the sink to flush it through, and it should be clean, sparkling and odour free. As a reminder – our drains and sewers were designed only for liquid and human waste, yet over time they have been subjected to an assortment of other waste materials that can easily contribute to small blockages at home and bigger problems in the wider sewer system and oceans.

Avoid sink blockages

To avoid blockages, slow flow and smelly sinks, as well as do our bit to help save our sewer workers from unpleasant tasks and consider the well-being of our fishes and planet, the following should never be put down the household drain via sinks, waste disposal or toilets.

Flour

This, I think, was my mistake – a little flour, breadcrumbs, etc., I would throw into the sink and swill down, though in truth it probably didn't go any further than the plug hole! Flour will turn into a thick sludge that will grow in size as it collects further debris.

Grease, fats and oils

While they might look runny and free-flowing when still warm in the frying pan, roasting tin or dish, once cool grease, fats and oils have the potential to congeal and harden, coating the insides of pipes and resulting in slow-flowing sinks, smells and blockages. I pour used fats into an old cup that I keep just for the purpose, then once solid I remove them from the cup using a round-bladed knife and pop the solid mass into a used flour bag and into the refuse. A small quantity of used oil left in the frying pan is easily sorted. I add 1–2 tablespoons of washing soda to the pan, which soaks up the fat and cleans the pan at the same time. I then use a spatula or spoon to collect the solids, which I also transfer into a used flour bag to dispose of.

Coffee grounds and tea leaves

Small amounts may seem harmless as they easily swill down the sink and into the drain, yet apparently coffee grounds in particular can be one of the biggest offenders for blockages. In reality, they clump and bind together when wet and will refuse to dissolve or break down, leading to stubborn blockages. Avoid a hefty plumbing bill and pop them into the compost.

Pasta and rice

Grain products continue to absorb liquids even after they are cooked, and will do a great job of adding to a blockage problem. While it may seem okay to let a few rice grains go down the sink or push a few pieces of cooked pasta down the plug hole, beware they could end up being the major culprit. Most new sinks come with a small filter to pop over the sink hole that will capture any debris. If you don't have one, they are not expensive to buy and could save you a fortune in plumbing bills in the long run.

Small paper products

Paper items such as price tags, shrivelled jar and food labels may seem harmless enough, but due to their sticky nature they can readily adhere themselves to even the smallest collection of existing debris in sink drains, leading to a more serious problem further down the line. Bigger paper products, such as wipes, large amounts of toilet paper and nappies flushed down the toilet cause huge problems in the wider sewers. You have probably seen the disgusting fatbergs in city sewers and the poor workers that have the thankless job of manually breaking them down and then physically having to remove them in order for the nation's sewerage system to remain intact. Be sure to dispose of paper products into the general refuse.

Medication

While unused medication – those few dregs left in a bottle, tiny tablets and capsules – may not cause a drain blockage or odours, they can cause problems further down the line to marine and aquatic life. I read that filtering systems are not able to remove certain chemicals from our waste, and so these chemicals will end up being discharged straight into the sea. Unused or expired medication should be returned to the pharmacy.

Cleaning products

As green cleaners we know that proprietary non-eco products should never be put down the drain (or used at all). All we need to do is read the reverse label to be warned of the dangers to aquatic life. When I wanted to dispose of unused (non-eco) cleaning products I took my box to the local recycling centre where I understand licensed waste carriers arrange for disposal.

Paints

Whether water- or oil-based, paints should never be poured down the sink. Paints are usually classified as hazardous waste, and again, your local tip will have a place to leave paints, creosote, oils, liquid varnish, etc. Oil-based paint needs to be removed from brushes using white spirit, which is not eco-friendly or water-soluble. However, the white spirit can be used over and over. Him indoors has a bottle for used white spirit and after cleaning brushes using an old paint tin, he then pours the cloudy white spirit into a used transparent plastic bottle. After some time the paint solids separate from the spirit and sink to the bottom of the bottle. The clear spirit can then be poured off to be used again for the next brush cleaning. The paint solids in the plastic bottle are then disposed of. A pot of vinegar with a squirt of eco-friendly washing-up liquid can also clean up paint brushes thereby avoiding the harsh chemicals altogether.

Slow-flowing sinks

Sinks and drains can kick back at you by going on a 'go slow' if overloaded by too much soap scum, grease, food debris or hair products. The very old hand basin in my bathroom can periodically play up, as can other basins, especially at Christmas time when we have many guests and visitors who put them through lots of use (and maybe misuse).

The kitchen sink on occasion does not empty quickly and efficiently. I used to buy chemical-heavy de-bung products, which worked, of course, due to the harmful caustic soda that simply blasts its way through any obstruction. My original advice on this in my book *Clean & Green* was to use a hot washing soda solution, which you pour down the sink and leave for 8 hours, after which time the sink is free-flowing. This works well as it dissolves any grease and soap scum that may be lurking in the pipes.

However, an even more effective and quicker way is to call on our 'false friends' as a 'one off' to speed up the task. When 'green cleaning', we have learned that the mixing of an acid and an alkali creates a chemical fizz. This is great in baking because this action helps to make cakes rise, and when used in bath bombs as the acid and alkali come together in water the resultant fizz creates interest and fun, but the same does not apply when we use them together in cleaning. The result of the two chemicals cancelling each other out renders each one pretty powerless.

The sodium friends

Bicarbonate of soda, washing soda and green bleach (sodium percarbonate) belong to one group of friends. They work well on their own, are non-acidic and you will know them because they are in many recipes.

The acid friends

Vinegar, lemon juice and citric acid are friends together, too – all acidic, natural and very effective, with fantastic cleaning powers.

Should any of the sodium or acid friends meet or be mixed together, however, they fight – punching and screaming, fizzing and knocking each other around until all their energy is used up. Nothing is left, just a pile of salt. Add 1 teaspoon of bicarbonate of soda, washing soda or green bleach to 1 teaspoon of vinegar or lemon juice and watch the immediate chemical reaction take place. The fizzing and bubbling is fun to watch but absolutely useless in cleaning.

Sadly, I see so much false information on social media where people promote using this as a cleaning method. I have one exception, however, where this fizzing and bubbling can create a huge disturbance! For sinks we can bring the two 'false friends' together in the form of washing soda or bicarb and vinegar (or lemon juice), because as they fight and fizz away they agitate debris build-up, which is better than washing soda alone.

You will need

600ml (1 pint) heatproof measuring jug
wooden spoon
smaller jug or cup

150g (5½oz) washing soda or bicarbonate of soda
150ml (5½fl oz) just-boiled water
150ml (5½fl oz) vinegar or lemon juice

Place the washing soda or bicarbonate of soda into the measuring jug, pour over the just-boiled water and stir until you have a cloudy solution. Pour the hot solution directly down the plug hole, then follow with the vinegar or lemon juice.

You will probably hear the fizzing and gurgling as the two chemicals fight against each other. At the same time their agitation will help to dislodge the cause of the blockage – you may even see splashes of debris pop up out of the plug hole. Once the fizzing stops, pour down a kettle of just-boiled water to flush any debris away. The sink will be free-flowing once more.

Blocked toilets

A scary sight – the toilet is blocked. There is dirty water nearly up to the rim of the toilet. What is to be done? Don't call the plumber right away, you should be able to fix it yourself using an old mop! I have a very tatty one that hangs outside, come rain or shine, and is used very occasionally to clean the garage floor.

You will need

old mop
bucket of cold water
2 large black bin bags

Start by wetting the mop head in the bucket of cold water to give it weight. Lift the wet mop from the water and place it inside one of the black plastic bags, then hold on to the bag along with the handle.

Carefully place the bag-covered mop into the toilet, slowly so as not to cause the toilet water to spill. Once you feel the mop is at the base of the toilet, begin to make small plunging actions right at the base and into the U bend. A few repeated actions and the soiled water will suddenly disappear as the blockage is forced down the drain.

Lift the mop out of the toilet and use the second bin bag to cover the soiled one, then remove and dispose of both bags.

Flush the toilet and all is well without the need for blasting chemicals or a hefty plumber call-out fee. Unfortunately, here we have had the need to use single-use plastic bags, but I haven't found a way around that yet.

Bye-bye fly

Do we really need fly spray? I used to buy aerosol cans of it, close doors and windows and then spray the room. Oh my word, when

I consider the coughing fits I had afterwards there is no wonder they are considered harmful if inhaled. I have not used them for years, choosing instead to have metal-chain fly screens at the outside doors that are very effective.

Flies have a fantastic sense of smell and will buzz around sweet, sugary foods, including very ripe or rotting fruits, juices and alcohol drinks. The greatest fly attractant, apparently, is the banana – and I can certainly relate to that. During the summer months, an overripe banana in the bowl will have a collection of tiny fruit flies that make you wonder how they ever got there. The trouble is, flies go from filth to food in a short time and can easily spread disease, usually resulting in tummy bugs, though in worse cases it can be salmonella, cholera and typhoid. Although flies have the potential to spread germs and disease, there should be no problems encountered as long as good hygiene standards are maintained. For example, always cover foods, especially a cake or tray of biscuits, and store them in an airtight tin. Keeping uncooked foods in the fridge will ensure they stay fresh for longer and fly-free, and always be sure to wash salad leaves and vegetables before eating to get rid of any bugs.

I use my all-purpose spray (see page 10) to wipe down all surfaces before preparing food such as bread or pastry where I will be working directly on the work surface. Its anti-bac properties will quickly clear areas of grease, dirt and bacteria – leaving the area safe and clean.

I have fly screens at the doors, yet in the summer months the flies manage to come into the house through open windows. Flies hate the smell of lemon, especially if that lemon is studded with whole cloves. This simple little tip works for me, and I received so much positive feedback from many others when it was shown on national TV, so much so that supermarkets were said to be out of cloves for a while!

Do remember that flies are attracted to smells both pleasant and unpleasant, and so for this reason they are blighters when it comes to spreading germs. I recall one person contacting me to say that the lemon and clove hack just doesn't work. I asked whether there were any foods lying around, or full pet-food bowls. His answer to me was no but there was a full refuse bin in the kitchen waiting to be taken out. Once that was removed, with the lemon and cloves in place there were no more flies!

You will need

2 egg cups or shot glasses

1 fresh lemon

20 cloves

Cut the lemon in half crossways then stud each half with 10 cloves, one into each juicy segment and one in the centre for good measure. Then pop each lemon half into an egg cup or shot glass.

Leave the lemon halves near an open window or door. I keep one in my pantry and one in the kitchen.

I replace the lemon about once a week and reuse the cloves one more time.

Spent lemon and clove insect repellent

After using the lemon halves to repel flies in the house, waste not want not, I make use of them again as an insect repellent.

You will need

> glass jam jar with a screwtop lid
> witch hazel, to cover
> funnel
> 300ml (10fl oz) glass spray bottle
>
> 2 spent lemon halves, studded with 20 cloves

Place the dried lemon halves with cloves intact into the jar, pour over sufficient witch hazel to cover, replace the lid and leave in a cool place away from direct sunlight for at least a week. The witch hazel will take on a golden colour and will smell faintly of cloves and Christmas.

Using the funnel, decant the mixture into a spray bottle and use as an insect repellent before setting off on a country walk or popping out to do some weeding on those warm summer 'insect-biting' days. Make sure you do a patch test before spraying this all over your skin, and always avoid any broken or damaged areas.

KITCHEN TIPS

My favourite room – the kitchen! The busiest, most used, warmest and most welcoming room in my house. This is probably the case in many homes, and for the modern kitchen user there is always something that's going to take our fancy. Could it be time for a complete revamp, and the dream of having an ergonomically and professionally designed workspace complete with modern cupboards and surfaces, or, often the more likely and more affordable, an everyday new tool or gadget that may be grabbing our attention?

I have drawers and cupboards full of tins and tools, a mixer, bowls of all sizes, baking dishes and not to mention the utensils, sieves and scrapers!

I used to want the latest of everything with the expectation (and hope) that my cooking, baking and meal preparation would become more efficient and better, yet the truth has usually been that after a short time the novelty would wear off and I would go back to my old, faithful, much-loved tool kit. It is possible to run a good kitchen without the need for lots of kit.

When it comes to kitchen equipment, my advice is to think twice. Is this a want or a need? Are you being persuaded by advertising, and can the job be done without this gadget? Will it be used and have you the space? The best recommendations I have found come from other users, not the paid advertising.

Don't get me going about my ice cream maker, portable pizza oven, veg and fruit shredder and mini chopper – all gathering dust in the garage.

I don't want to knock all gadgets – there are some amazing little tools that I wouldn't be without. My simple cherry stoning tool and (wait for it!) a magnetic stirrer I received that keeps my milk stirring while cooling when making yoghurt, preventing a skin forming and resulting in a thick creamy yoghurt – now that was a great Christmas gift.

There are some items, gathered over the years, that I am steadily replacing, and these are my kitchen plastics and non-stick items. There is so much concern about plastics leaching from products such as chopping boards and plastic utensils, non-stick pans, casseroles and baking products, so I have decided that little by little I will replace these pans, baking tins and trays in my kitchen with cast-iron and stainless-steel versions. My plastic utensils and boards will be replaced with glass, metal and wood. Glass boards for meat, fish and chicken; wooden boards for bread, fruits and veggies; and utensils made from wood or stainless steel.

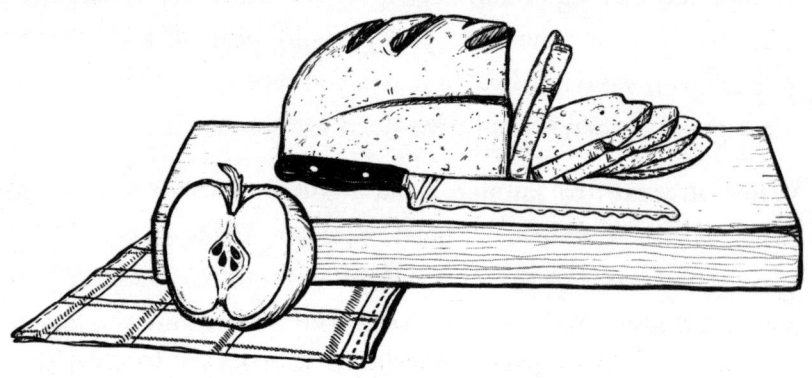

When I first embarked on my green journey and began mixing my own products I saved plastic spray bottles and containers that had originally housed the chemical-heavy products. I hadn't really considered the plastic packaging until it dawned on me just how much of it I *wasn't* now using. The plastic recycling bin (collected every two weeks) was now seldom full – no coloured bottles and plastic wraps. This really was a win-win. As the original bottles I was using no longer felt right for me – they were too big or too small, or the spray attachments failed to operate – I replaced them with glass. I never discard glass jars and bottles, as I know there will always be a use for them.

I can, of course, remember a time when there was little plastic used in packaging – always glass or paper. Milk came in glass bottles delivered by the milkman daily, sweets and confectionery sold loose in paper bags, meat and fish wrapped in wax paper, and when it came to fish and chips, simply newspaper and fingers, not a polystyrene tray and plastic fork.

I still carefully wash the inevitable and unavoidable plastic trays and containers that come with my food shopping and add them to the recycling bin, but at the same time feel a huge sense of achievement that my single-use plastic consumption has been reduced considerably and that my little life isn't adding to the massive plastic pollution problems that we have.

Glass, on the other hand, has been around for centuries, is 100 per cent recyclable and is made from three natural ingredients: namely sand, soda ash and limestone. My collection of jars and bottles have a whole range of uses. I store foods, syrups, pickles, jams and liquids in glass – whether that be in the fridge, pantry or freezer. Glass is robust and can withstand temperature fluctuations, so, yes, it can stand boiling water, it can stand the freezer. The only reason it cracks in boiling water is if it has been shocked. Glass is fine coming up to the boil as long as it started from cold. Glass will not crack in the freezer as long as the contents have been given room to expand. As liquids freeze they expand, so if they don't have sufficient space in their container they will push the glass and cause it to crack. Ever put a bottle of wine in the freezer to quickly chill then forgot about it? Most likely the bottle will have cracked because as the full bottle freezes, the wine inside has nowhere to expand and so cracks the glass. When freezing in glass – jam, gravy, sauces, for example – I leave about 2cm (¾in) headroom in the jar.

Unlike plastic, glass will not absorb staining or odours from foods, so it can be easily cleaned and used for different things. It will not leak microplastics into food or into the waterways. Any limescale deposits that can form on glass vases and drinking glasses can be easily removed using a spray of Pure Magic (see page 7) scrubbed with an exfoliating glove.

I have had many messages from people asking me to sell my products 'ready-made' to save the job of having to mix them oneself. My reply is always – what about the packaging? Inevitably, more plastic would be involved, there would be the cost of manufacture, labelling, marketing and supermarket space. Much better we do it ourselves and bypass this unnecessary packaging and cost. We can reuse our own bottles at home, know what is going into our products, choose to buy ingredients in bulk to reduce packaging and decide what works best.

As an aside there are products being sold in 'paper' packaging such as pouches, bottles and bags promising to be biodegradable. In truth, everything is biodegradable – the question to be asked is how long will it take? A plastic bottle is biodegradable, it just might take a few hundred years. Messaging is misleading for the consumer, but we want to believe what we're told.

Let us take, for example, a paper bottle or pouch. At first glance and touch one assumes the packaging is what it says it is because it looks and feels like paper, but in fact there is a plastic lining on its inside. So, it is paper, but there is plastic too, which means this is yet another example of 'green washing' – where we are led to believe an item is eco-friendly, but the reality is that it will also end up in landfill, adding to the already massive microplastic problem. The word we should be seeking out is 'compostable' – if we see this we know that our packaging can actually go onto the compost heap, where it will decompose quickly and naturally.

My own efforts are a 'work in progress'. I realize there is a lot to do and it is not practicable or affordable to ditch everything at once, so with this green overhaul in mind I decided to critically examine my kitchen and pantry space and offer up some cleaning magic!

The big pantry clear out

I love my pantry and am so fortunate to have a walk-in area where I can see at a glance where everything is. I would like to say that I tidy and clear it out once a year, but the reality is that the last clear-out is often three or four years overdue – yet the feeling afterwards? Wow. Fantastic! I continued to pop in for days afterwards just to have a look around.

I chose a rainy day for this job, which had been nagging at me for months. I couldn't easily put my hands on what I wanted, and I remember needing a jar of capers, couldn't see any, so dashed out to buy them to then find an unopened jar tucked away in a corner when I was actually looking for something else – cornflour, I think!

That was the catalyst; there was nothing else for it, everything was due a clear-out. I decanted each item from the pantry into the kitchen next door. I was amazed that the items stored in this small, shelved room could go on to cover every work surface, my large table and even sections of the floor.

There were dust-covered yet perfectly good, unopened tins, bottles and packets, along with half-filled packets of dried fruits, flours and sugars. as well as near-empty jars of pickles, jams and sauces. There were also those containers of bizarre and unusual foods, bought for a specific recipe, used once and never used again – parma violet syrup, for one!

The pantry carcass was a sight – the shelves were very grubby in parts, marked with rust rings from old tins, spills from syrups and the most stubborn stains that had built up over the years. I even found, to my delight, an old yet beautiful stainless-steel frying pan, which I returned to its former glory (see page 138) and is now in regular use.

To get things back up to scratch, I cracked open my green cleaning tool kit. Maybe your kitchen cupboards are regularly emptied and cleared out, but if, like me, you've a situation on your hands, these are the tricks that transformed my pantry and got it sparkling in no time.

For rust rings, use a spray of Pure Magic (see page 7) and sprinkle over some table salt. Leave to soak for 10 minutes or so and the rust will dissolve. Wipe clean with a damp cloth to avoid any sticky residue when the Pure Magic dries.

Stubborn marks from oils can be easily cleared with cream cleaner (see page 11), which is more effective when used with a dry rather than wet cloth. I then use 2–3 tablespoons of Basic Magic (see page 43) added to a bucket of hot water to clean dirt and grime from each shelf.

Bear in mind I had a major job on my hands – if I had been more organized and had not allowed the shelves to become so badly covered in dust, dirt and grime, my all-purpose spray cleaner (see page 10), which is always my first port of call for a maintenance wipe and clean, would have done a quicker job.

Once the room was clean and bright, I then sorted through the foods and decided I would smarten things up – no more half-filled plastic packets. I chose to use glass jars, as I have a huge stock of these, and using a marker pen I labelled the contents as I filled them with nuts, seeds and dried fruits.

By the way – best-before dates on dried foods such as pasta, rice, lentils, spices, herbs and beans don't have to be rigidly obeyed. The quality of those dried foods may not be quite what it should, but they will be safe to eat. A pack of rice, for example, that had a best-before date of earlier on in the year was returned to the shelf, but put to the front to be used next in line. I am of the generation that managed before sell-by and use-by dates were added to packaging, so if something looks okay and smells okay – I am sure it is okay. I rely on my senses rather than dates, and my own children still gasp when they see me cut off the mouldy bit from hard cheese (not soft creamy cheeses) and discard it, then use the rest in a quiche, or use a large spoon to remove a speck of mould from the top of a jar of jam, bin it, then boil up the rest to use in my jam tarts.

People have been guided by their own senses of sight, taste, feel and smell for centuries before becoming reliant on dates on packs. However, if in any doubt – throw it out!

Just like in supermarkets, it is important to rotate foods kept in the house, whether that be in the cupboards, pantry, fridge or freezer. When examining the dates on my pantry goods and returning them to the shelves, those with the longest best-before date went to the back and the oldest foods came to the front to be used next. The tendency, especially when we're busy and need to unpack the supermarket shop as quickly as possible, is to put the newest purchases to the front. They are then at the top of the drawer and become the first to be used. Unfortunately, the older foods that stay at the back will continue to gather dust, and will be the last to be seen, so they may never get used and will end up being cast aside and added to the tons of rubbish in landfill. Try to get into the habit of rotating home stocks of foods.

The items I use the most were returned to the shelves at eye level (flours, sugars, oils, tins, eggs), and within easy reach, whereas those foods that were not used as often went to the top shelves, such as the bottles of spirits that only come out at Christmas.

I had nuts, seeds, rice, lentils, dried beans and dried fruits all in glass jars, my home preserves (jams, pickles, chutneys and sauces) neatly stacked, then sugars and flours stored in one place. My pantry was now a thing of beauty – no longer cluttered, foods in neatly labelled jars, no part-used packets, and everything easy to see and access. Why did I leave it so long?

It was nothing short of perfect – I love it!

Reusable piping bag

I am a lover of beeswax wraps made using pieces of muslin, and I think every book I've written introduces a new use for them. I started out using them as an eco-swap for cling film. They are great for covering bowls of food for the fridge, wrapping cheese and sandwiches, are safe for the freezer and, most of all, are washable, reusable and compostable. I then went on to make a wax bread bag with these wraps, for better and longer storage.

I used to use the oven to heat the beeswax to make my wraps, but in addition to the valuable energy that needed, it can get messy and, obviously, very hot. I also found I was using more wax than was needed and the beeswax tin couldn't be used for anything else afterwards – the thin coating of residual wax was nearly impossible to remove, and of course it can never go down the sink.

I then had a bit of a brainwave and decided to use my iron to melt the beeswax onto the fabric, using greaseproof paper. Less energy is used this way and the amount of wax needed is reduced because you can see what is going on. While I was at it I introduced a reusable, washable piping bag. Back in my non-green days I used to buy single-use plastic piping bags on a roll – tear one off, use it, then throw it away without another thought to the end of life of that item. I now know it would end up in landfill or be incinerated.

Hefty linen, reusable piping bags were the 'go-to' when I was a child – I think I remember my grandmother having one, though it was a bit unsightly, as I recall. I think it was a bit yellowed and smelly, though maybe that is a distant memory. Reusable cloth piping bags are now available, but on close inspection many of these have a thin coating of plastic on the inside. So how about a beeswax, reusable, washable, naturally anti-bac piping bag? I love mine – it's better than paper because it holds its shape, doesn't leak and after use is simply unfolded, washed, dried, quickly refreshed and reshaped, ready for its next use.

To make two you will need an exact square of very thin cotton. I choose white and, rather than buy new, it is handy to reuse thoroughly clean old cotton sheets or pillowcases that have worn thin and would be otherwise added to the 'dust sheet' pile. I use 100 per cent cotton for a few reasons – firstly, being a natural fabric it is compostable and, once it has had its day, can be tossed onto the compost heap to break down naturally. Beware cotton and polyester mixes, as these contain man-made fabric that will not break down in the same way. Secondly, 100 per cent cotton, when used for food piping, will not leach any harmful chemicals into the ingredients, whereas polyester mix may just do that. Thirdly, 100 per cent cotton can withstand high temperatures when ironing on the beeswax, unlike polyester blends which often melt under a hot iron.

You will need

a square of cotton of any size you prefer, but start small – maybe 25cm (10in) square.
scissors
iron
greaseproof paper
100g beeswax pellets (sufficient for two piping bags)
2 pairs tweezers (optional)
cardboard tube (from a used roll of kitchen paper)

To coat the fabric

Press the cotton square so that it is completely crease free, then fold it corner to corner to make a triangle, then press again. Cut along the pressed line so that you have two identical triangles of cotton.

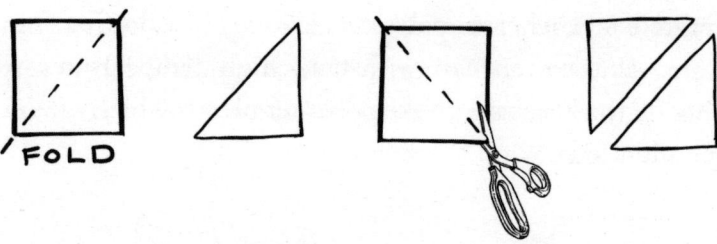

Lay a length of greaseproof paper onto the ironing board, making sure it is larger than one of the triangles of cloth. Sprinkle over the beeswax pellets evenly. Each pellet will roughly double or treble the space it occupies on the cloth, so try to space them evenly. Cover then with a second piece of greaseproof paper.

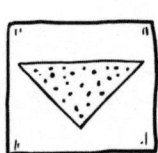 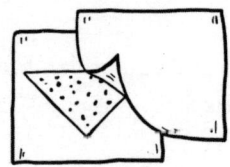 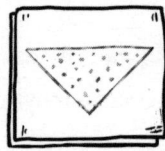

Heat the iron to medium without steam and gently iron on top of the paper. You will see the wax soften and then melt and be absorbed by the fabric. While hot, lift the paper and add extra pellets if you see a gap in the wax.

Once you can see that the fabric under the paper has changed colour as it has absorbed the wax, turn off the iron. While still hot, and minding your fingers, peel off the top layer of paper and then immediately the warm, wet, waxed cloth.

Hold it up using two hands (or use tweezers if you don't have heat-resistant fingers like me), and pick it up by two corners of the triangle so that it doesn't fold in on itself. Within a minute the wax will have cooled and stiffened and the fabric can be laid onto a work surface. Repeat with the second piece of fabric, adding more wax as for the first one.

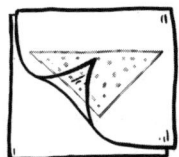 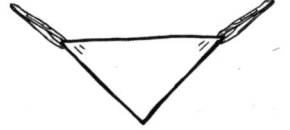 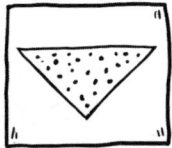

Any cold wax left over on the paper can be easily peeled off and added back to the bag of wax pellets. Roll the pieces of greaseproof paper and secure in a cardboard tube (I mark my tube 'beeswax') as they can be used again next time and for refreshing.

To make the piping bag

Place the triangle of wax fabric in front of you, with the point nearest to you and the flat side furthest away. Take one of the sides and fold it inwards, forming a cone shape. Repeat with the second side, only this time the end folds around the back of the cone. Both points will be next to each other and can be secured by simply bending over – the fabric, stiffened by the wax, ensures the bag remains in a sealed position. The cone shape can then be fitted with a piping nozzle or used as it is, then popped into a large glass and filled with cream or buttercream, etc. After use, unfold, wash in warm soapy water and air dry.

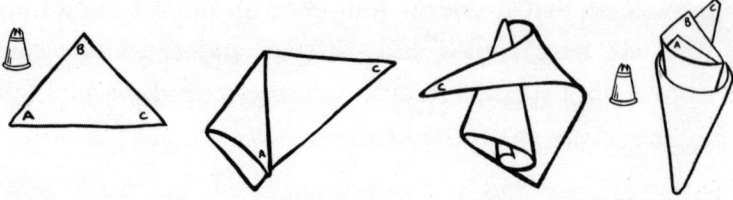

If the piping bag is very creased it can be quickly refreshed next time the iron goes on. Lay between the two sheets of greaseproof paper once again and iron over to smooth out the creases. No need for extra beeswax. I re-form mine into a cone shape so that I have them ready to go next time they are needed.

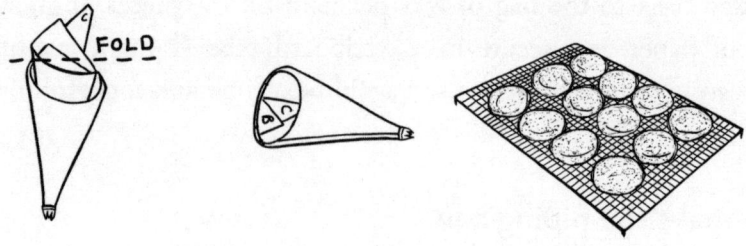

The stainless-steel pan

I am gradually replacing my non-stick pans, particularly frying pans, with stainless-steel or cast-iron versions. The reason being that non-stick pans can easily chip and scratch, which means they are not especially durable and long-lasting. Warnings are now being circulated that damaged non-stick pans should not be used because their scratched coating can cause food to be contaminated by PFAS (per- and polyfluoroalkyl substances, some of which may contain a class of chemicals whose use have been restricted in the EU).

I remember the joy when the non-stick frying pan came into my house. A fried egg slid around without any sticking, not much oil needed, and this was just great. Over the years the coating got scratched when a metal tool was inadvertently used instead of the plastic one, and it was not until I read the warnings that I decided to go back to basics.

My damaged non-stick pans of all kinds (of which there were quite a few), have now left the house. I have a stainless-steel frying pan that was too good to throw away when it was replaced by a new, modern, better (so I thought) non-stick type. My good old stainless-steel pan with a very stained copper bottom had been tossed to one side, forgotten about, unloved and confined to a dark corner of the pantry.

Some years later I carried out a big pantry clear-out (see page 129), which was well overdue, and I re-discovered my stainless-steel frying pan. Not used for at least 20 years. I remember thinking at the time that it was not fit for purpose because all food stuck to it, but I now realize it was me that was at fault – not the pan.

Stainless-steel is fantastic. A good pan compares in price to a non-stick pan of the same size, will last a lifetime if looked after properly, will not chip and will not prove harmful to health as it doesn't corrode. My cookware of choice is now stainless-steel, cast-iron, ovenproof glass and enamel. Finding a pre-loved piece of stainless-steel cookware is great and there are many bargains out there.

My pan was stained with burnt-on food splashes, as it had not been properly cleaned after its last frustrating frying session, and it was very dusty and dirty, with even a thick cobweb knitted around the handle for good measure. So this is how I cleaned mine.

You will need

large sink or bowl
fine wire wool

2–3 tbsp washing soda
just-boiled water
bicarbonate of soda
Pure Magic (see page 7)

Start with an overnight soak. Place the pan in a sink or bowl big enough for it to be fully immersed into, sprinkle over the washing soda, then pour over just-boiled water until covered and leave overnight.

The next day the majority of the burn-on debris will simply wipe off. Clean any remaining stubborn areas easily using dampened fine wire wool dipped in dry bicarbonate of soda. The copper base of my pan was badly stained, but a spray of Pure Magic left on for 20 minutes, then rubbed with the fine wire wool cleaned the base up a treat. The pan looked like new again.

Non-stick without the non-stick coating

Obey a few simple rules and your stainless-steel cookware will not stick – I now look forward to frying eggs in mine!

Place the dry pan over a high heat. After a few minutes add a drop of water – if it fizzes and evaporates the pan isn't hot enough. Leave the pan to heat for a further few minutes, then add another drop of water – this time it should glide around the surface of the pan looking like tiny glass pebbles or a single mercury ball (this is called the Leidenfrost effect). The pan is ready and will now essentially act like a non-stick pan.

Allow the water to burn off before adding any fats. The pan is now very hot, so turn down the heat, leave for a minute or so, then add your oil or fat of choice. I use 1–2 tablespoons of olive oil in a 25cm (10in) pan for frying eggs. Some prefer butter.

TOP TIP: I crack individual eggs into a cup before adding them to a pan. Many years before dates appeared on eggs, I cracked a bad egg straight into a pan with three others that were not bad. Result? Four wasted eggs. I now always crack each egg into a cup before combining them.

The eggs will cook beautifully without sticking. Use a metal slice to ease the egg from the sides. Some like to flip their eggs, some prefer to baste, but if you have used little oil for frying and not sufficient to baste – a lid (glass, if you have one), placed over the pan will enable the surface and the yolk to cook from the steam within the pan.

KITCHEN TIPS • 141

Perfectly fried eggs, no sticking and a pan that can be cleaned easily without burnt-on residues. Maintaining and cleaning your stainless-steel cookware is a breeze!

White spots and water marks on stainless steel

When boiling water, maybe for soft- or hard-boiled eggs or pasta in a stainless-steel pan, the minerals from the water (particularly for those living in hard-water areas) may leave tough residual stains in the form of white rings and white dots on the base and sides of the new, shiny pan. The pan, even once washed and cleaned, looks dull, unsightly and definitely not new anymore.

Thanks to Pure Magic (see page 7) this can be sorted immediately. Just one squirt left for a minute will clean any mineral deposits without the need for scrubbing or scouring. Spray it on and, using a damp cloth, wipe away any marks – water stains will disappear, leaving your stainless-steel pan looking clean and shiny once more.

If you don't have Pure Magic made up and ready, a spent lemon half rubbed over will do the same thing, but it may take longer and need a little elbow grease.

My stainless-steel milk pan

When non-stick bakeware, pans and products were introduced I loved them – particularly my small milk pan. At long last milk could be boiled and the pan simply rinsed and wiped clean.

However, for the reasons stated above I now have a stainless-steel milk pan that isn't as well behaved. In addition, I use a large stainless-steel saucepan to boil 1 litre (34fl oz) of whole milk to make my own yoghurt. The pan afterwards is coated with a stubborn layer of thick residue that is very difficult to remove, needing time, patience, hot soapy water and a scouring pad. This little tip will save all of that faff.

After boiling your milk, swill the pan using cold water, tip it out to remove any milk residue, then sprinkle over about 1 tablespoon of washing soda and sufficient water, hot or cold, just to cover the base of the pan – usually around 3–4 tablespoons. Leave to soak for around 15 minutes, that's all, then you can take a cloth to the pan and it will clean up without effort.

Seized washing soda (sodium carbonate)

From the day I decided to go green there has always been a kilogram pack of washing soda in the house. However, I now shop in bulk and buy huge tubs of my green cleaning staples. Washing soda (sodium carbonate) has so many uses in cleaning, laundry, odour neutralizing, path cleaning – the list continues to get longer.

However, have you ever picked up your pack to find it solid as a rock – brick hard? This may be due to moisture, but more often than not it is because the washing soda has been subjected to excess heat, probably during storage. I remember a few summers ago the temperatures exceeded 42°C (107°F) in the UK, which is very unusual, and I noticed that one effect was that so many packs of washing soda in the supermarket were rock solid.

Even though my bulk tub in the garage was fine, I decided to buy a pack to try to remedy the problem. Information online was to dissolve the brick with hot water and use it as a liquid, but that seemed like an awful lot of solution to store, and I prefer my washing soda to be in powder form so that I can calculate dosages accurately, etc. So this was my solution to the problem.

You will need

large, roomy mixing bowl
wooden spoon
rubber gloves

1kg (2lb 4oz) brick of washing soda

Place the unwrapped brick in the large mixing bowl and leave it in the fridge overnight. The next day, use the handle of the wooden spoon to break pieces from the brick that have softened due to the cold temperature. Pop it back into the fridge for another day.

Next day use the wooden spoon handle again to break the remaining lump into small pieces then, wearing rubber gloves, rub the remaining lumps between the fingers (as you would when making pastry by hand) until the washing soda has returned to powder form. Transfer to a tub with an airtight lid and it is ready to use.

Big fridge and freezer clean and tidy

This is done twice a year in my house. Firstly I do this in the run up to Christmas, when I know I need the space as I will be making and storing extra food to get ahead. My second tidy up is during the lean lull of early summer, when my frozen home-grown produce is coming to its end, or just before harvest time when I know I will need space to freeze fruits and blanched vegetables.

I am lucky enough to have more than one freezer, because I love growing and storing a lot of my own fruit and vegetables. I make an extra effort to use up what is in one freezer for some weeks before a clear-out, then transfer any produce from the other freezer into it. If I see half-packs of unused frozen fruit, I will put them all together, weigh them, thaw them and make jars of jam. My empty freezer can then be switched off and allowed to thaw in its own time. I lay dog towels at the base of the freezer to soak up water and leave the door open while it defrosts, otherwise odours quickly build up.

You will need

- hot water
- cloth
- paintbrush
- cardboard box
- bowls and pans
- old towels or clean dog towels

hairdryer (optional)

eco-friendly washing-up liquid
small bowl of bicarbonate of soda
cream cleaner (see page 11)
green bleach foam (see page 63)

When the inside of the freezer is clear of any ice I can start to clean. I use only eco-friendly washing-up liquid and hot water. Any stubborn scuffs or marks can easily be removed using a wrung-out, warm, damp cloth dipped into a little dry bicarb. Occasionally there may be very stubborn grey water marks on the back wall of a freezer or fridge and the dry bicarb will remove these quickly and without effort.

Examine door seals too, because these can harbour dirt and mould – a damp cloth and cream cleaner will quickly wipe those clean. Very stubborn mould stains on door seals can be removed using my green bleach foam painted on and left to do its magic.

If you have one freezer and it is not possible to decant the contents into a second freezer, while you thaw and clean, things can be sped up. Work at reducing the contents of your freezer beforehand so that there are not huge quantities, then get to work. Switch off the freezer at the mains then remove the contents and place them all together in a cardboard box in a cool place. Once the freezer is empty, fill bowls and pans with very hot water, place these onto the freezer shelves and close the door. Soon you will hear chunks of ice falling from the shelves.

After half an hour or so, open the door, place some old towels at the base of the freezer to mop up water as the ice melts. Carefully remove the loosened, thawing chunks and pieces of ice and put them into a bowl to then tip outside. Don't be tempted to force stubborn ice with metal instruments because you could damage the freezer.

If the freezer is very ice-packed it might be necessary to repeat this, though usually one session is sufficient. Any stubborn ice areas can be released quickly using a hairdryer.

Once all the ice is away and the freezer is looking bare and clear once again, wash down as already described – there always seem to be a few stray peas! Dry the shelves thoroughly before putting everything back and switching on the machine, as any areas left wet will quickly turn to ice.

Pack the frozen foods back into the various compartments, checking that everything is labelled and dated. There's no point in putting something back that has no identity.

Switch on the freezer and keep the door firmly closed until it reaches temperature.

NOTE: Never use proprietary, heavy-chemical cleaning sprays or materials that could later release harmful substances or transfer odours to the food.

KITCHEN TIPS • 147

Labelling is so important

Sometimes I have something that needs to go into the freezer and I think I will remember what it is later, so I simply add it to a freezer box or bag without any date or label. The huge disappointment then when I thought I was taking out a frozen tub of gravy to serve with a savoury pie, only to discover it was leftover caramel sauce to serve with sticky toffee puddings. I have done this so many times in the past that I have now learned my lesson.

Now, I keep frozen fruits together, then meats, fish, vegetables and freezer jams. I grow most of my fruit and vegetables, and when I enjoy a good harvest year there will be bags of blanched veggies to freeze and store. I batch-cook for the freezer, too, so that I always have casseroles, pies, fillings, cakes and breads. My life is very busy now so I have to be sure I can put my hand on something quickly for a meal when I am working. I think it is so important to date my frozen foods as well as label them, so I can keep a rotation system going and use up my older produce first. My freezer is one of my best friends! I know there are some very organized types who manage to keep an active list of what is in their freezer – I am not at this level, though it would be handy.

Freezer odour

Freezer odour can develop due to foods not having been stored or wrapped correctly, or maybe a food has been kept too long and has developed a rancid odour that then permeates the freezer. I have had messages from those in distress because owing to power cuts or freezers that have suffered a fault, they have been left with spoiled foods and an awful freezer odour, even after cleaning. Spent lemon halves boiled in a pan with water can be removed from the water once cooled and left in the clean freezer to help neutralize any residual smell. I have found the best odour prevention is fresh air, though, so whenever a fridge or freezer is not in use, always leave the doors wide open.

I am not sure what the culprit was, but there was a time when my whole freezer developed an odour.

I have an ice maker in the door of my freezer that dispenses ice cubes into a container, which are very handy to pop into drinks, especially during warm weather. However, on one occasion, in the middle of a gardening session when all I called for was a glass of ice-cold water, I poured myself a welcome glass and added a handful of the said ice cubes. Instead of quenching my thirst, it had the opposite effect because there was an unpleasant taste to the water – I could best describe it as a cross between fish and garlic. Not great at all. The smell was the same and I wondered whether it was the glass I was drinking from. I knew it couldn't be the water, so I changed the water and the glass, added more ice cubes then realized that here lies the problem – the ice cubes!

I returned to the freezer, unclipped the ice maker from the freezer door to discover the whole unit carried the same unpleasant odour, and because I now had the smell fixed in my nostrils I could smell it everywhere when I opened the freezer door. I am uncertain as to why this happened – the ice cubes had obviously absorbed an odour from something in the freezer, and thinking back it could have been from a mammoth batch of fresh fish I'd added. I had laid each fillet out on trays to open freeze before packing them into bags and containers.

The plastic icecube compartment was taken outside, ice cubes discarded onto the garden and the unit left in an open position in the fresh air for two days.

To absorb and neutralize any residual odours in the freezer

You will need

> small bowls or saucers – one for each shelf
> 2 tbsp bicarbonate of soda for each bowl

I added dry bicarb powder to small bowls – 2 tablespoons in each – and placed one bowl on each shelf and into each drawer of the freezer and left them in there for two days. This may have been overkill, but I didn't want to have to remove all the foods, thaw the freezer and start again.

Thankfully, the odour disappeared in less than 24 hours, though I left the bicarb in there for longer. Lesson learned, so now, once made, I pack ice cubes into their own container if I plan to open-freeze any foods.

Once removed, the bicarbonate of soda used did not go to waste. I added it to a sugar shaker and used it to sprinkle over and clean the kitchen sink for a few days to come.

Dishwasher detergent

At last – I think I have sorted this recipe for *everyone,* as I know so many readers are understanding more and more that the chemical-heavy proprietary products are really not great for the environment and there is some suggestion that residues may be left on glass, crockery and cutlery. Who knows? Some people adore my original recipe, telling me it gives great results and there is no going back. Others (particularly those in very hard-water areas) really struggle – the glasses have a cloudy residue, water-stained cutlery and some tea and coffee stains remain.

Before we begin, ensure your dishwasher filter is clean and clear, the machine is topped up with salt (if this is a requirement of the model you have) and the interior settings are adjusted per the manufacturer's guidelines according to the water type you have.

I will explain further, but I have found it better to break dishwasher detergents into three options based on water type. If you are unsure of your water type, an online search may advise based on postcode or your water supplier. In simple terms, if your soap lathers well, then your water is soft, if you achieve few suds then the water is often hard.

Option 1 – soft water

Original detergent. In a jar, mix 100g (3½oz) green bleach, 300g (10oz) washing soda and 100g (3½oz) bicarbonate of soda. Use

2 teaspoons of the mix in the detergent dispenser plus 1 tablespoon of vinegar in the rinse aid compartment, per cycle.

Option 2 – hard water

In a jar, mix 360g (12¾oz) bicarbonate of soda and 120g (4¼oz) green bleach. Use 3 teaspoons of the mix per cycle in the detergent dispenser (each cycle needs a ratio of roughly 2 teaspoons of bicarb to 1 teaspoon of green bleach). Plus 1 tablespoon of citric acid in a metal tea strainer on the dishwasher shelf and 1 tablespoon of vinegar in the rinse aid compartment, per cycle.

Option 3 – very hard water

Follow the same procedure as above, using 3 teaspoons of the detergent mix and 1 tablespoon of vinegar, but use 2 tablespoons of citric acid in the tea strainer per cycle rather than 1 tablespoon.

To use

As above, mix the chosen detergent recipe in a jar (the green bleach and bicarbonate of soda and washing soda, if using) or, to start with, trial a smaller quantity until you know the mix works for your machine and water type. Don't add the citric acid to the detergent because the acid and alkaline mix will soon fizz then go solid and clump as they cancel each other out. This is a kind of 'pay as you go' detergent.

As an aside, I don't put saucepans into the dishwasher, preferring to wash them by hand. The reason for this really is that they take up far too much space. I prefer to hand wash a large casserole dish and save my dishwasher for cups, plates, glasses and cutlery. Repeated use of citric acid can dull enamel on pans, so follow the manufacturer's guidance for your precious pans and oven dishes. For those that say I am using more water to wash the dishes by hand – I use the same bowl of soapy water for wiping down worktops, the table, cooking spills, the oven and hob after cooking as I use for my pans and dishes, so no extra water is used. Cleaning down is part of washing up – the dishwasher cannot do everything.

TIP: Never put sharp knives in the dishwasher, for two reasons. Firstly, the dishwasher will blunt the knives, and secondly, it is suggested we stack our cutlery with prongs and spoon upwards, so a sharp, pointed knife stacked this way is certainly a recipe for danger and injury.

When the machine is full and you are ready to go add 2 or 3 teaspoons of detergent (depending on water type and mix chosen) to the dispenser and close the flap. Add 1 tablespoon of vinegar to the rinse aid compartment and close the flap. If using, add 1 or 2 tablespoons of citric acid to the tea strainer on the top shelf – I pop it amongst the cups, mugs and glasses. The aim of the tea strainer is that it will ensure a slower release of citric acid throughout the main wash cycle.

I choose a hot 70°C (160°F) cycle – mine takes just over 2 hours. A short wash and the cool but long eco wash cycle just don't give clean consistent results in my machine, but experiment with what works best for your individual make and model. There should be no cloudy glasses, no water marks on cutlery and plates and cups are stain-free. No limescale build-up or deposits, and the citric acid is a natural deodorizer too.

I live in a very hard water area and have been using option 3 for over a year without huge problems, though I do have 2 large mugs where I think the glaze must be worn off because they always come out of the machine stained with tea or coffee. I have to grin and bear it, though, and clean them up using 1 teaspoon of bicarb and a damp cloth. I can cope with this slight inconvenience knowing that none of my drinks or plates of food are at risk of contamination from any residual harmful chemicals left from proprietary products and I am not having to do the washing up by hand. I sincerely hope you can find a detergent here that works for you.

GENERAL HOUSEHOLD TIPS

GENERAL HOUSEHOLD TIPS

I thought I would give a mention here to those general household chores that I do, probably without knowing exactly when the routine actually started and that have become second nature, but also very useful.

I would like to start with those chores that require water, partly because I for one tend to take it for granted, yet during recent times warmer summers and longer dry spells have me thinking about water usage, water wastage and being savvy about just letting it run down the drain.

No water waste

Here in the UK, we tend not to worry about our water supply, partly because it seems to rain all the time. However, when we do get a dry spell it is not too long before we are being asked to be careful about our water usage. Our constant on-tap, 'always there' water supply should not be taken for granted and I try to be sensible over my water usage. Here are some ideas to help you save water that work well for me.

When I want hot water in my kitchen sink, I measured that I run off at least 3 litres (5 pints) of cold before the hot comes through. I used to just let it run down the sink and onwards into the drain.

This is good water, so now I always use this as an opportunity to fill the dog's drinking bowl, or the washing-up bowl ready to wash veggies, salads and the like, and I also fill a small watering can that I use for houseplants.

I regularly swill my dog yard with leftover floor-cleaning solution, washing soda soaking solution and any clean rinsing water. It's a great job on a warm, dry day – just swill the solution around straight from the bucket, work it in well using a stiff yard brush and leave to dry.

I collect rainwater to water my growing veggies, but I use it in cleaning, too, especially those outside cleaning jobs that in the past I may have used water from the tap, such as cleaning down patio furniture, plant pots, my greenhouse – the list goes on.

In summer, it seems that increasingly often we have a very hot dry spell and a directive can come from the water companies not to use a hosepipe in the garden, and to use water sparingly, filling up watering cans for essential watering of plants. On one such summer, thankfully, my veggies had a dwindling supply of rainwater left in the water butt, so they would be okay for a bit, but my rose beds, planters, pots and borders, on the other hand, were suffering. The clay soil had large cracks, the leaves and flowers were wilting and my containers were bone dry. There was no rain in the forecast, either. I cast my mind back to the drought of 1976 and got out the hosepipe, as I remembered the television and radio advice back then: bathe with a friend, place a brick in the toilet cistern to ensure less water is used, flush the toilet less often and use bath water for the garden by syphoning it off through a hosepipe.

Rather than take two separate showers where the water would leave the house and go straight into the waterways, instead I ran a bath. I took a shallow bath and after a day in the garden a hot soak was most welcome. I added Epsom salts to soothe my aching muscles – plants love it too. The second bath was taken by 'him indoors' using my water – he needed to top up with a little more hot. The bath water, rather than let out by pulling on the plug, was instead siphoned off and used to water my plants.

This really was a trip down memory lane. The hosepipe roll was taken upstairs into the bathroom, one end laid into the bath and tied with string to the tap by the plug. The rest of the hosepipe was passed out through the window and down to the yard below. The hosepipe end in the yard was then attached to an outside tap and switched on. The water travels up the hosepipe until it reaches the water in the bath above. Someone in the bathroom will give the signal that water is coming into the bath. At that point the tap is switched off and the hosepipe disconnected from the outside tap. Be ready at this point, because without any hesitation the hosepipe will flow water through at a good speed while it does the job of draining the bath of its contents. If you don't have a handy outside tap, a good suck on the hosepipe will bring the water through too!

I enjoyed 20 minutes of watering of my pots, containers, hanging baskets and borders before the bath drained completely. I was happy and so were my plants.

I have since discovered that there are grey water diverters available that will do the job for you. A diverter can be fitted to bath waste at high level, which diverts water down a standard hosepipe and into a water butt to provide year-round water for the garden. Even more reason to be mindful of what is going down your plughole – and to go green!

The bins

Single-use plastic bin liners were used extensively in my house. Weekly, there was a small bag for the bathroom bin, medium bags for the two bins under the sink and a huge thick black one contained all of the contents from the bins already mentioned. When I considered the amount of single-use plastic bags leaving my house each year, multiply that by the number of houses in my street, then the town as a whole – not to mention extrapolating to cities and countries – the enormity of the plastic waste problem hit me in the face. I decided to start small with just my house, and stopped using bin liners.

I realize some local authorities insist that household waste goes into bags and I feel sorry that this is the case. Once again, I remember a time before plastic bin liners existed and when it was important to dispose of household waste carefully in order to keep your galvanized dustbin clean and odour-free. Food waste was always wrapped in newspaper, as was any other refuse that may spill.

This was an easy swap to make. I keep paper flour and sugar packets and plastic bags that may have contained other items. Rather than going into the waste bin empty, they are used to hold items that could leak, make a mess or smell.

Not only did I decide to dispense with bin liners, I decided to give my bins a thorough clean, too. My wheelie bin really was a sight – grubby on the inside and on the outside were a number of half-peeled-off stickers that had been stuck on some years back explaining when the Bank Holiday collections would be. I needed to be proud of my bin.

I would like to boast that I clean my wheelie bin regularly, though in reality I only manage to get around to it about twice a year. Here's how I do it.

You will need

> bucket of hot water
> long-handled, soft sweeping brush
> old pastry brush
> sticky label remover (see page 58)
> expired credit card, wallpaper or bench scraper (for scraping)
> cardboard
>
> 1.1kg (2½lb) washing soda
> a few drops of essential oil

On a dry day, add the washing soda to the bin, pour over the bucket of hot water, then using the long-handled brush work at the base and sides. This solution can be left in the bin to soak for a few hours and dissolve any stubborn debris, then simply tip it on its side and let the water pour away. I have a gravelled drive, so the solution can pour off with no harm to the environment.

For those without a space to tip the cold washing water, I would be inclined to walk my wheelie bin to the nearest road gulley and pour it down. Then give the bin a rinse with clean water then leave it on its side to dry in the fresh air.

The ugly stickers on the lid of my bin were tackled next. Using an old pastry brush (that I now keep secured with an elastic band with the jar of label remover), brush the label remover (see page 58) over the lid of the bin and leave it to soak in for around half an hour. An expired credit card is the perfect tool to scrape off the labels.

My bin looked gorgeous! Finally, before putting it back into use I laid a square of cardboard in the base to help protect my super-clean bin from future stains and added a few drops of essential oil to the cardboard to give a pleasing perfume each time the lid is lifted.

The bins under the sink

I have two – one for kitchen waste that cannot be composted at home, and the other for green kitchen waste that goes straight onto the compost.

The kitchen waste bin is not too difficult to keep clean because I make sure that waste matter is wrapped in old packaging and newspaper before I add it, but the compost bin, by comparison, can look disgusting.

This plastic bin with handles takes the lot, including coffee grounds and tea leaves mixed with vegetable and fruit peelings, as well as the odd eggshell, and the results are a fairly ugly and soggy collection. Once tipped onto the compost, where Mother Nature will carry out the natural transformation from yukky to yummy, my bin still looks very yucky. This bin, unlike the large wheelie bin, is thoroughly cleaned each week.

You will need

very hot water
old sink brush
cloth

2 tbsp washing soda
2 tsp green bleach
cream cleaner (see page 11)

Place the washing soda and green bleach into the bin and pour over very hot water. I usually do this to at least half way up as this is the grubbiest area.

Leave to soak for at least an hour – I leave it outside, swirling the solution around using an old sink brush from time to time.

Any stubborn stains can be removed using a blob of cream cleaner and a cloth, though usually the soak is sufficient. A sheet of newspaper or brown packaging paper laid into the bottom of the clean, dry bin helps to contain future staining. Just change this each time you empty the bin.

Mop cleaning

As I have mentioned in other areas of this book, I consider the 'end of life' of everything that I buy these days. I used to buy a well-known brand of floor mop with a microfibre mop head. I thought it was great – it could be squeezed out to almost dry so I could mop my floors with ease, then I could unclip it and pop it into the washing machine with my cleaning cloths. Over time the mop gathered bobbles (obviously collections of plastic) and the mop head looked tired and worn, but no worries as I could buy a replacement to clip onto the end and off I went again. The metal handle rusted at the end and eventually became detached from the plastic clip that held the mop head.

Only now do I realize that the worn mop head, plus the obsolete plastic clip, once discarded from my house, would add to the pile of refuse going into landfill, and the plastic pieces and microfibres will stubbornly remain in place for decades before they eventually decompose.

My final microfibre mop was used and never replaced; instead, I bought a wooden-handled mop with a head made of string. There is no plastic clip-on/-off attachment and no metal pole that will rust. My sustainable mop, however, cannot easily be removed from the wooden handle, so rather than using the washing machine I keep it white, bright and free of odours as follows.

You will need

1 bucket
boiling water

2 tbsp washing soda
2–3 tsp green bleach

Better results are achieved when cleaning a dry mop head rather than one that's already cold and wet. So, place the dry mop head into an empty bucket and sprinkle over the washing soda and green bleach, then pour over a kettle of boiling water – sufficient to cover the mop head. The solution will froth as the green bleach is activated, so gently move the mop around in the solution to make sure the many cotton fibres are well submerged. Leave to soak for 6–7 hours, after which time the green bleach will have decomposed into water, soda ash and oxygen.

Squeeze out the mop using the bucket's wringer – the residual washing soda solution can be used to swill a path, clean pet areas or imitation grass. I prefer to find a second use for it rather than pouring it down the drain.

Pour clean water over the now clean and bright mop head and agitate it in the bucket. Continue to rinse until the water is completely clean, then hang outside to air dry.

Never leave a wet mop in a bucket of water, because any metal parts will rust. Similarly, a wet mop left in an empty bucket will smell in a matter of days. Left to hang outside at all times, it never gets unsightly or smelly. I have a screw on the outside wall specifically for my mop. After use, I wring it out and leave it to dry naturally – come rain or shine. The mop dries without knots and without odour.

When my mop eventually comes to the end of its life (and so far it has outlived any of the plastic alternatives), the mop head can be unscrewed, cut up and composted and the wooden handle reused with a replacement mop head.

In the future, when my plastic buckets eventually crack or break I will replace them with a metal mop bucket.

Lambswool fluffy

I have used all manner of gadgets over the years to brush cobwebs away. I live in an old house and spiders love it here. I have never tried to eliminate the spiders because I am convinced that they keep me clear of other pests. Spiders not only eat flies, but they also feast on moths, earwigs, ants, woodlice and centipedes, and are natural predators of silverfish. I don't have a houseplant aphid or fruit fly problem because my army of spiders, I am sure, are always at the ready!

While I want to protect my spiders, equally I don't want the house of Miss Havisham, so the webs need to be kept at bay. I use a natural lambswool fluffy on a long pole to periodically whip away the cobwebs, and it does the job very well indeed.

The cobwebs are sticky, often grey in colour, and may have a few insect skeletons thrown in for good measure. So over long use the lambswool fluffy is no longer soft, white and gorgeous, but grey, dusty and unsightly. So how to get this looking white, bright and fluffy again?

You will need

rubber gloves
bucket
warm water (not hot)
wide toothed metal dog comb

2 tbsp wool detergent (see page 206)
2 tbsp fabric softener (see page 200)

I do this job outside. Wearing rubber gloves, stroke the cobwebs from the lambswool. The sticky silks will leave the wool and adhere to the rubber glove – it really is quite satisfying. Be sure to remove as many cobwebs as possible, because once wet they are very difficult to loosen.

Then take the bucket, add the detergent and sufficient warm water (not hot, you don't want to shrink your fluffy!) to fill the bucket to about two-thirds full. Agitate the fluffy in the water using your hands. The dirt will dissolve away, returning the wool to its clean natural state.

Squeeze the wool, then plunge it into a bucket of clean cold water containing the fabric softener. This solution will dissolve any residual soap and leave the wool soft and fluffy.

Now the fun bit – take the pole of the lambswool fluffy between both palms and swizzle it back and forth. The lambswool will release so much water and fluff outwards in the process. Imagine a wet dog giving itself a shake – it gives off much more water than can be dabbed with a towel. This is the reason I do this job outside.

Leave the fluffed-up lambswool to dry outside, and when almost dry use a wide-toothed metal comb to tease any tugs or residual pieces of cobweb, leaving the fluffy as good as new.

Sheepskin rugs

I have had a number of requests about the best way to clean a sheepskin rug. They are white, soft and fluffy when new but then the wool gets grubby and unsightly, especially if knots begin to form. One particular problem comes to mind when I recall a follower feeling she would need to throw her beautiful lambswool rug away because a sick dog had stained the rug badly, leaving nasty stains that remained even after a clean-up. Rather than throw it away, we decided to try this instead.

You will need

wooden spoon
wide-toothed metal dog comb
very hot water

2–3 tbsp wool detergent (see page 206) or washing soda (for stain removal)
1 tsp green bleach (for stains and to whiten and brighten)
2–3 tbsp fabric softener (see page 200)

Note: If the rug needs only a clean rather than stain removal, I would just use 2–3 tablespoons of the wool detergent and the green bleach. Washing soda can be harsh on wool.

This is best done in the bath or a large basin. Add the wool detergent (or washing soda if badly stained) and green bleach to the bath and add enough very hot water to dissolve the solution. Stir with a wooden spoon until the solution has dissolved, then add cold water to fill the bath to about 25–30cm (10–12in) deep. The water needs to feel tepid in temperature (neither hot nor cold).

Give the rug a good shake outside to remove any dust, then lay it wool-side down and skin-side up in the water. Push it under the water using the wooden spoon, then leave to soak overnight.

Next day, empty the bath water then push as much solution out of the rug as possible by pressing down on it with your hands, then add cold water to the bath along with 2–3 tablespoons of fabric softener. The fabric softener will help to soften the wool and dissolve any residual soap.

If the rug can fit into the washing machine, pop it in there for a very quick spin (see tip on spinning woollens on page 209) to remove excess water, otherwise leave to drip-dry outside.

As the rug is drying, shake regularly to lift the wool and tease out any knots using a wide-toothed comb. I use a metal dog comb, which does a great job. Following the above treatment your rug should be much improved and almost like new.

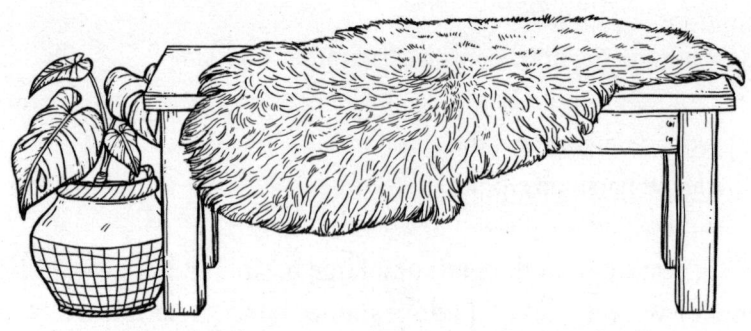

Window blinds cleaning

Many people have been in touch about how to best clean vertical and Roman blinds. They may have water marks, mould spots or just have been in place a long time, and rather than having to go to the expense of replacing them, they are willing to try anything I can recommend.

A number of people have used this method and have been delighted that the blinds are once again clean and bright, and they have saved money by not needing to replace them. I have used this method to clean 'dry clean only' Roman blinds with water marks and mould. Absolutely delighted that I avoided a chemical-heavy clean at the dry cleaners.

You will need

> very hot water
> wooden spoon
> large bowl or bucket
> cloths
>
> 200g (7oz) washing soda
> 4 tsp green bleach
> all-purpose spray cleaner (see page 10)

This is best done in the bath or a large basin.

The vertical panels or blind (in a folded position) can usually be unhooked from the blind fitting. Take these outside and give them a brush or a shake to remove any excess loose dust and cobwebs, etc.

In the bath, add the washing soda and green bleach and enough very hot water that you can stir the solution around until it dissolves. Then add cold water to fill the bath about one-third full. The temperature needs to feel tepid (neither hot nor cold). Lay the vertical blind panels or folded blind in the solution and leave overnight to soak.

Next day, rinse well using regular changes of cold water, then take them from the bath, turning vertical blinds panels loosely into a coil (no folds). The more bulky Roman blinds can be upended in a bucket then taken outside to drip dry.

While the blinds or panels are air drying, use a cloth and all-purpose spray to clean the frame, strings, etc. Once dry, hang back in place.

If you are worried about colour runs or whether your blind can withstand a wash – test a small area in a large sink. Wash just one panel using maybe 1 tablespoon of washing soda and half a teaspoon of green bleach.

Preparing to decorate a room

Have you decided to take the plunge and redecorate a room? Maybe you have decided to save some well-earned cash and take on the task yourself. If the walls are already painted, before diving in with a brush and new paint have a think about them. If it is some time since the room was redecorated, if there were smokers in the house and central heating or wood-burning stoves, it is likely those walls will be grubby and greasy in places, and if not washed first, the paint may not give an even cover when applied.

The first job, after clearing the room, is to wash the walls and paintwork to remove grease and grime, and if you have stripped wallpaper then a wall wash is recommended to remove any old residual wallpaper, paste, grease and dirt. There are products on the market that promise to do this job quickly and without the need to rinse. Many are expensive and contain harmful chemicals – we can do the job just as efficiently and very cheaply using our home-made products.

You will need

bucket
hot water
sponge or cloths
rubber gloves (optional)

4 tbsp Basic Magic (see page 43)

Add 4 tablespoons of Basic Magic to a bucket, then add the hot water and use the foamy solution to effectively cut through grease, grime and remove loose debris. Depending on the size of the room and the amount of dirt, you may need to change the water regularly, but that's not a problem – Basic Magic costs a few pence to make. Wipe down, squeeze out the cloth regularly and there's no need to rinse the walls after.

The big car clean-up

I know there are many people out there who are so precious about their cars and will only use the proprietary products recommended by the manufacturer. You only have to browse the specialist stores to see the range of products available – something for every nook and car crannie! For those wanting to clean their car using home-made natural products and achieve a good result, read on.

Bodywork solution

You will need

bucket of hot water
cloth

200ml (7fl oz) white vinegar
50ml (1¾fl oz) eco-friendly washing-up liquid
10 drops of essential oil (optional)

Combine all the ingredients, adding some essential oil for perfume, if you like. Dilute 2 tablespoons of the solution in a bucket of hot water when ready to use.

I use this cleaner diluted as directed to clean the car bodywork to remove mud stains, water marks and insect marks, and on the aluminium wheels. Rinse off using clean water followed by a thorough polish with a wash leather to prevent streaks. I use this on the windscreen and windows, too.

Interior dashboard

On the inside I use my all-purpose spray cleaner (see page 10) on dashboards and any plastic areas around the doors, glove compartments, etc. Spray and wipe with a dry cloth – it dries quickly without streaks.

Leather upholstery

I use my cream cleaner (see page 11) and a dry cloth to remove any stubborn stains. I find the most difficult stains are easier to remove if cream cleaner is used on a dry rather than a damp cloth. Once the stain is lifted, a wipe over with a warm, damp cloth will remove any surplus product.

Fabric upholstery

I use my dry-ish clean recipe here (see page 60). After cleaning, be sure to leave car doors and windows open to ensure the interior dries completely, otherwise a fusty smell may develop.

Bumps, scratches and bug stains

Cream cleaner (see page 11) (non-abrasive and non-acidic) used with a dry cloth can remove many unsightly scrapes before anyone is any the wiser, and used with a wet cloth it will remove even the most stubborn fly and insect marks.

Headlights

Use cream cleaner (see page 11) to sparkle up yellowed or cloudy glass, which builds up on car headlights.

Soft-top roof

I don't have a soft-top car, though many people have used 2 tablespoons of my bodywork solution diluted in a bucket of water and applied it with an old sink brush to clean up the most stained, green and badly neglected soft top. Scrub the warm soapy suds into the fabric to clean, then rinse with clear cold water and leave to dry.

Car carpet stains and spills

After brushing out or vacuuming car carpets there may be a residual stain or spill or simply dirty marks from shoes.

You will need

large bowl or bucket.
cloths

2 tbsp bodywork solution
200ml (7fl oz) tepid (not hot) water

In a large bowl or bucket, dissolve the bodywork solution in the tepid water. Dab at the stain with a cloth dipped into the solution, working from the outside inwards until the stain has gone. Leave the car doors and windows open to allow air to circulate and the carpet to thoroughly dry.

Nature's freebie – air freshener

A dangling air freshener swinging from the rear-view mirror is the trigger for a headache, especially when the weather is warm and the synthetic chemical perfumes tend to be even more pungent. If you feel the same and don't want to breathe in the toxic fumes, but equally want a fresh smell during your driving time, along with a free gift at the end, try this.

You will need

- cotton drawstring bag, organza bag, laundry zip bag or a paper coffee filter
- handful of fresh mint or rosemary leaves or small bunch of lavender

Fill the chosen bag with your natural herbs or flowers and place it in the car, or line the cup holder with a paper coffee filter and add a handful of fresh herbs. I am not too keen on a bag swinging from the rear-view mirror – I think it can obstruct the view and become a distraction. Instead, I fill the bag and leave in full sun on the dashboard – it works just the same and the heat from inside the car and particularly on the dashboard will release the aroma and dry the items out at the same time.

Enjoy the natural perfume until such time as the flowers or herbs have dried. Once dried, decant into jars to use to make lavender bags or dried herbs in the kitchen. Much cheaper and more enjoyable than a dehydrator.

A regular squeeze or scrunch of the bag will do two things: first, it will release a boost of perfume, and secondly it will help you to judge how dry the herbs or flowers are. A crispy scrunch and they are about done – a soft scrunch and they will last a bit longer.

Going on holiday cleaning checklist

At last, the time has come – you have probably waited all year for a much-needed holiday in the sun. Alternatively, you may be leaving the house for some time because work calls you away, or you may have property that is rented out and there is a checklist that needs to be followed to ensure everything is ship-shape before the next people arrive.

I follow this simple checklist, knowing I am then unlikely to come home to any unwanted surprises.

Dishwasher

After the unload of clean pots and dishes, check the filter and give it a clean, then run a hot cycle using 100g (3½oz) citric acid to clean, sanitize and deodorize. Use a folded tea towel to hold the door slightly ajar to allow air circulation while you are away to prevent any odours building up inside.

Washing machine

Leave the detergent compartment and door to the drum wide open to prevent mould and odours.

Turn off the water

Turn off water at the mains, then there is no fear of returning home to a burst pipe or leak.

If you are going away in the winter this is particularly important, though check that your heating is a closed system that will not need extra water if it has to come on if the temperature drops below freezing in the house. There will be a 'stop tap' for the house to close off all incoming water – mine is in the toilet downstairs and the tap turn is very stiff, so it's worth having a practice before the day of departure.

Kettle and iron

Make sure there is no water left in the kettle or the iron. Leave the kettle lid slightly at an angle to allow air circulation. Leave no water in the iron – it can build up limescale and end up shortening the life of the iron.

Dishcloths

Soak the cloths in a mixture of 1 teaspoon of green bleach and boiling water until cool enough to handle, then hang over a tap to dry out. Never leave a wrung-out dishcloth at the side of the sink, as it will turn smelly and develop mould spores.

Houseplants

When holidaying during the summer months I stand my houseplants outside in a shady spot. Your plants will receive a welcome wash down and shower whenever it rains. Even if the weather is dry while you are away (unlikely in the UK), the plants will still take moisture from the air outdoors and you may have a friendly neighbour who is happy to keep an eye on them – especially if you make life easy for them and leave a full watering can alongside.

Laundry

I try to leave home with a full suitcase and an empty laundry basket, because I know the machine will have a marathon session on my return and I don't want dirty clothes from before I even set off to add to the load.

Fridge

Check the fridge for any perishable items that won't last until your return. If you have been well organized you will have used up foods and not replaced them. There may be butter, bread, milk or cheese, and if you are in any doubt, pop them into the freezer and take them out on your return home. Even a minimal amount of surplus milk can be frozen in an ice-cube tray, then you know you have enough for a cuppa on your return until you get the chance to do a shop.

Toilets

I give toilets a final clean and flush, then spray them with Pure Magic (see page 7) to prevent any limescale build-up while I am away.

Infused vinegar

'I want to go green, I know vinegar is a great natural cleaning product, but oh – the smell!'

This is the feedback I get from many people who don't like a vinegar smell when it's used as an ingredient in my cleaning products, or even when used on its own.

Instinctively, we add more perfumed essential oils to try to mask the smell, though I have found that this doesn't really help and in any case I am now using essential oils less and less – they are expensive and some are not great around pets.

There are odourless cleaning vinegars on the market, and others that promise lemon and eucalyptus-type scents, which may be slightly more acidic (around 10 per cent acid) than the food-grade, distilled white vinegar (just 5 per cent) found in the supermarket. They will also be more expensive, and as my objective is to be spending less, I have yet to splash out and buy specific cleaning vinegars.

Citrus-infused vinegar

Using my budget 5 per cent, food-grade, distilled white vinegar from my local supermarket and rather than discard orange, lemon, grapefruit or lime skins and peelings, I simply pack them into a large glass jar, top up with the vinegar, seal and leave to infuse for 2–3 days. You will achieve a tinted vinegar that will have taken on the colour of the fruit skins along with a pleasing citrus scent rather than that of the pungent vinegar.

Leave the vinegar even longer – 2 weeks or so – and the vinegar will be very dark in colour with a more concentrated scent. Pour the infused vinegar through a tea strainer to filter out and remove any small fruity bits that may have left the skins.

Use citrus-infused vinegar in any of my cleaning recipes that use vinegar.

All-purpose floor cleaner and car cleaner

Combine 200ml (7fl oz) infused vinegar and 50ml (1¾fl oz) eco-friendly washing-up liquid, then add a couple of drops or orange, lemon or lemongrass essential oil, if you like.

Fabric softener

Combine 200ml (7fl oz) infused vinegar, 15ml (1 tablespoon) vegetable glycerine and 10 drops of eucalyptus essential oil (for a lasting laundry freshness).

General polish

Combine 30ml (1fl oz) infused vinegar, 50ml (1¾fl oz) oil of choice (the thinner the better) and Magic Mixer (10 drops polysorbate 80 or 1 drop honey or glucose).

All-purpose spray cleaner

Combine 60ml (2½fl oz) infused white vinegar, 150ml (5fl oz) water, 40ml (1¼fl oz) surgical spirit and add 10 drops of your favourite essential oil, if you like.

Odourless surgical spirit/rubbing alcohol

There are odourless surgical spirits available, which is good to know, and these can be found online. Some choose to use cheap vodka as an alternative.

Infuse your surgical spirit, rubbing alcohol or cheap vodka in the same way as we have the vinegar above. Fill a jar with lemon or orange peels, pour in the surgical spirit, put the lid on and leave to infuse for 2–3 days. Again, like the vinegar, the alcohol will take on a coloured tint and a citrus rather than a clinical smell. Use neat as a disinfectant on surfaces or as an ingredient in other recipes, including my all-purpose spray cleaner, above, and Easy Breeze fabric spray, see page 235.

Reed diffusers

Over the years I have been gifted many reed diffusers; a pretty package containing a bottle of perfumed oil, 6 or 8 reeds and the promise of a natural room fragrance.

At one time in my life, I had a number of them around the house, though I have to say once they lost their perfume (and their appeal) they tended to gather dust. I would forget to flip the reeds regularly in order to refresh the 'scenting' effect and at one time when I did I allowed the upturned oily reeds to touch my wallpaper, staining it permanently.

The oil inside the bottle tends to discolour in time because it doesn't all evaporate, and although I held on to the attractive little bottles, for me, reed diffusers had gone out of fashion.

I decided to put the pretty glass bottles back into circulation as I realized I had a collection of essential oils in stock. I could buy a bottle of carrier oil and new reeds, then I would be up and running again.

However, for the reasons explained I didn't want to invest in carrier oil. Oil-based reed diffusers were just not for me. Instead, with my new Magic Mixer ingredients (see page 14) and their emulsifying properties, I was able to develop a recipe and make a water-based reed diffuser. I just needed to buy new reeds – cheap as chips.

The benefits for me of home-made diffusers are many: using water is much cheaper than buying a carrier oil, the contents of my 100ml (3½fl oz) bottle evaporate in about a week and there is no manky looking oil after many months of neglect, and when I turn the reeds (usually daily to release fresh scent) any spills are harmless. Oh, yes – and I get to reuse my pretty little bottles!

The ingredients below make enough scent for a 100ml (3½fl oz) bottle, so scale up or down accordingly.

You will need

an old reed diffuser bottle or small-necked jar or vase
glass jar with a screwtop lid
small funnel
6–8 reeds

100ml (3½fl oz) water
10 drops of essential oil of choice (try lily of the valley
　or honeysuckle)
Magic Mixer (10 drops polysorbate 80 or 1 drop
　honey or glucose)

First of all, fill your diffuser bottle with water to find out how much it holds, then pour this into the screwtop jar. Add the essential oil of choice and Magic Mixer of choice. Screw on the lid, give it a good shake to emulsify, then use the funnel to transfer the liquid to the bottle or vase of choice.

Add 6–8 reeds or as many as can be fitted into the narrow neck, leave for a few minutes for the reeds to soak up the scent, then flip them over to release the perfume and enjoy the subtle, natural and not too strong scent in your room.

If you forget to turn your reeds, the ends left in the solution can appear grey in colour, but don't worry, once turned and exposed to the air they will dry and return to their original state. With this in mind, when going on holiday I remove my reeds from the liquid, which may well go on and evaporate if away for a long time. The reeds can then be added to new solution on my return.

If you forget to remove them and your reeds become unsightly, don't despair. Lay them in a shallow bowl, add a teaspoon of green bleach and cover with boiling water to soak then air dry – they'll be as good as new.

Wild flower seed waste-paper gifts

The inspiration for this little project came together one spring – the sun was shining, I had been spring cleaning and tidying out my study, it was my birthday and there were seeds to be sown outdoors. How did these various events lead to an idea?

Let's start with my study clear-out. I had A4 diaries going back some years, in which I scribble recipe ideas – some fully worked up, some scribbled through – as well as notes of phone conversations and diary events. I really considered I was becoming a hoarder and these had to go. Secondly, it was my birthday and my son had gifted me a super little card with his usual 'Happy birthday Mum' – he's not a man of many words. However, he did write inside – 'read the back'. I turned the card over to see that the paper was handmade and had been embedded with seeds. It was advised that the paper be cut into squares, laid on dampened compost, watered regularly and the seeds would germinate. Thirdly, it was springtime and I had just bought some other seeds for the year, including wild flower seeds. Fourthly, we were in for a few days of dry, warm sunny weather, so what better time to have a go myself?

I used wild flower seeds in my gifts, but any small, easy-to-germinate seeds will work. Mixed salad leaves or annual bedding flowers are great, for example.

You will need

Waste paper, shredded or torn into small pieces
large bowl
shredder (optional)
warm water
plate to fit the top of the bowl
blender with blade attachment or food processor
seeds of choice (see intro)
board, baking sheet or tray
old towel or tea towel
thin piece of cotton fabric
large spoon
small, angled palette knife
wire cooling rack
rolling pin
ruler
Stanley knife
scissors

optional extras

food or soap colourings
needle and thread
pressed flowers

Use as little or as much paper as you have. I used 3 very large handfuls of shredded paper and placed them into a very large mixing bowl. If you don't have a shredder, the paper can be torn into small pieces. Pour over sufficient warm water to cover – the paper quickly sinks into the water.

Ensure the paper is under water, then cover it with a plate to keep it submerged and leave to soak overnight. The next day the soft paper can be transferred in soggy handfuls into the bowl of a blender or food processor. Note of caution – do not overload your mixer! I did just that and pebble-dashed the kitchen work surface, the floor, the oven door behind me and even the dog asleep in his bed! So, working with small quantities at a time, blitz until a thick pulp is achieved. Mine was a very pale blue, tinted due to the blue fountain pen ink I use when writing, which I liked. If you want to colour your white paper, add a few drops of food or soap colourings when blitzing.

Once I had a large bowl of paper pulp, I added my seeds. I used two packets of wild flower seeds, each containing 50 seeds, but one packet will be fine. Stir them into the mix then you are ready to make the paper.

I made two large sheets as follows. Lay out a solid board, tray or baking sheet and cover with the old towel, which will absorb the excess water. Lay over a thin layer of cotton (this will ensure your finished paper has a flat, smooth finish) – I had fabric remnants of curtain lining, which were perfect.

Using the large spoon, transfer half of the mix over the thin fabric – about six spoonfuls filled the area – then use the palette knife to smooth it out into a thin even layer without any gaps or holes. The angled palette knife was perfect to tidy up the edges, leaving me with a large, tidy rectangle of pulp. From the paper pulp I achieved two A3 sheet sizes.

The sun was shining, making the perfect conditions to get the pulp to dry quickly. As the pulp dries it stiffens, and I was able to slide away the board underneath it and replace it with a cooling rack so that air could get to the underneath as well as the top surface.

After 5 or 6 hours in the sunshine my paper was almost dry, so to complete the smooth finish I slid the paper from the cooling rack onto a solid surface (still on the cloths) and rolled and flattened it to make it even thinner using the rolling pin. The paper was now smooth, very thin but still damp.

Left overnight in the house, it became perfectly dry. To remove from the cloth without fear of damage, flip the paper over onto the cooling rack and peel the cloth away from the underside. If it is still slightly damp, leave to dry out completely on a flat surface.

I cut my paper into squares, choosing to score strips first using a ruler and Stanley blade. The smaller strips were then easier to handle and cut neatly using scissors. I cut pieces, each about 5cm (2in) square, made a hole in one corner using a needle and thread to make a loop so that it could be hung and to add a little interest, then stuck a pressed flower on one side using a blob of edible glue to secure.

I made up a collection of 50 little seed paper gifts decorated with pressed primroses, forget-me-knots or daisies (all in flower at the time I made them) and added one to every family or friend's birthday card with instructions for use.

I hosted a summer lunch with friends – there were 14 of us and I tied a little seed card around each serviette and they were a great talking point and a little home-made treasure they could pop into their pocket and take home to plant later. My table centre was a small pot of compost with germinated seed paper, each collection of seeds being about 1cm (½in) tall at the time.

They last at least two years (the life of the seed) – probably longer.

Instructions for use

Lay the square of seed paper in a small pot of moist compost. It can be covered with a light layer of compost if you like, but there is no need. I quite like to see the paper come to life. Water well and keep moist at all times. Seeds usually start to germinate within 10–14 days, depending on ambient temperature. Leave on a light sunny windowsill, in a greenhouse or outside in summer. Once the seedlings have grown too large for the pot, transfer to the garden or outside space.

A great one for the kids to do, too.

CLOTHING AND LAUNDRY CARE

Clothing – a small word yet, it manages to successfully cover so much!

The human body, unlike other species, needs protection from the elements and extra layers to keep it warm. Other species have all of that built in and don't have the need for clothing because they have natural protection from their fur, feathers or scales.

We used to be covered in much more hair, but then environmental changes and, I read, a dissipation of body heat resulted in humans needing more protection from clothing layers. Studies have shown that wearing clothing dates back from between 83,000 and 170,000 years ago, when analysts first found evidence of clothing lice that had diverged from head lice.

This is so interesting! However, I shall stop digressing and fast forward to today, where clothing is a huge industry.

We all need and wear clothing to keep us warm, to protect our skin from the elements – and clever cuts and use of colour and different textiles certainly improve how we look.

The big wardrobe refresh

I remember reading somewhere that if an item of clothing hasn't been worn in two years then it needs to go. What?! I have garments I have had for much longer and I still love and wear them. I have a crepe black and yellow blouse that I bought back in the 1990s, I still wear it (minus the shoulder pads) and I cherish it.

I make some clothes – jumpers, dresses and trousers – and if any stitchers are reading this then you'll agree that if you have spent hours making something you will be reluctant to ever throw it away. Fast fashion is a modern word and an equally modern dilemma. So much clothing hits the market at an alarming rate, is affordable and so is mopped up, often by teenagers wanting to be seen in the latest styles. They therefore become an easy target for the fast-fashion suppliers' marketing campaigns. I was the same, once upon a time – I would dearly love to have had a new dress to wear on Saturday night (the only night I went out). A new dress would cost half of my wages but a length of fabric a lot less. The weeknights were therefore spent sewing in readiness for my next night out – when I wasn't attending night class to improve my shorthand and typing skills. However, nowadays fabric can be more expensive than the clothing available to buy, which is such a shame. Maybe there are fewer dressmakers out there, and because clothing is so cheap and 'throwaway' we have so much wastage and a huge problem of disposal. I now buy very few clothes – I really do have enough.

Whether it is because of my age, my growing conscience about the planet or simply a diminishing lack of interest in clothes shopping (preferring instead to be wearing my gardening gear and be outside) my wardrobe and drawers are still very full.

A few years ago I decided to check things out and tidy up how I kept my clothes. My jumper drawers were especially haphazard – with a few laid on the top and no idea what was underneath. Everything came out, then I folded them, rolled them and replaced them in the drawer in one single layer so that every jumper, cardigan and woollen could be seen. This was great. I did the same with underwear and a huge collection of scarves, folding and rolling them so I could see in one layer in the drawer what I had.

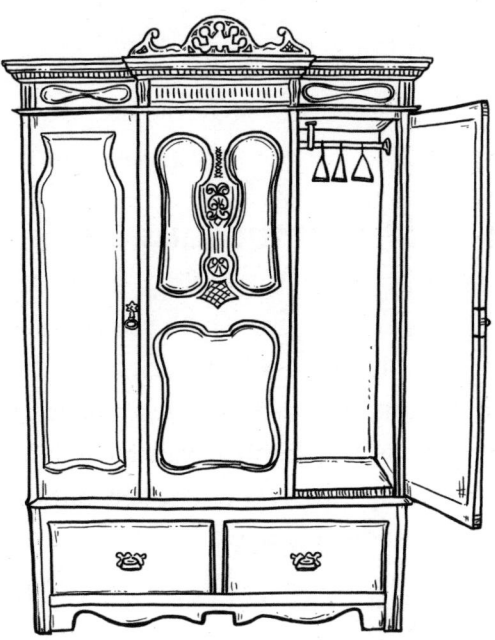

My wardrobe, too, was crazy. My double wardrobe is a huge, free-standing, Edwardian piece of dark furniture with a central full-length mirror. I bought it from an auction house several decades ago when we moved into our Edwardian house. The trouble is, back in those days people had fewer clothes – they were handmade, much more expensive, no fast fashion then, and therefore a single hanging rail would be all that was required even in the finest house. My clothes were stuffed in so tightly onto this single rail that it was sometimes difficult to part the garments.

Time for a clear-out, though not to throw them away – I sorted out the bulky winter clothes and moved them into the wardrobe in the spare room. Why had I not thought of this before? Summer and winter clothes divided meant I had sufficient space. My problem was solved.

See moth repellents, treatments and how I keep my jumpers safe on page 228.

Diatomaceous earth

Not easy to say and even more difficult to spell – this is an inexpensive, naturally occurring, fine powder made from the fossilized remains of tiny, aquatic organisms called diatoms. They apparently lived in prehistoric times, had silica-based shells and their deposits can now be mined.

I keep a large (inexpensive and food-grade) tub of this natural, non-toxic, fine, dark grey powder in the shed and use it for so many preventions and treatments if necessary. I have read it is also used in pool-filtration products, exfoliating cleansers, foundation make-up and toothpaste!

I use it as a natural insecticide; it works by drying out insects and their larvae. Perfect therefore for sprinkling on carpets both as an occasional prevention measure and a treatment, if necessary. It will treat bed bugs, get rid of flies, ants, cockroaches, fleas and ticks.

I dust it on my dogs to guard against fleas and ticks rather than using chemical sprays and tablets, and I use it routinely in my henhouse amongst the nesting material, sprinkling it into their 'dry bath' areas to ensure feathers and housing are always clear of red mite.

Anyone that keeps hens will know that an infestation of red mites is a living hell for chickens, and in severe infestations can kill them. Red mites are blood-sucking parasites that live in the coops and feed on the blood of chickens at night. They conceal themselves within the chicken coop surroundings and reproduce quickly, adoring the dark, moist warm conditions.

Again, not until there is a problem do we ask the questions and, just like a clothes moths issue, it took a red mite infestation for me to understand how much easier it is to prevent them than to treat. During the summertime when red mites will visit I do everything that these bugs hate. I open the doors, removing the nesting material and perches, allowing the sunshine and fresh dry breeze to blow through. I dust regularly with diatomaceous earth and keep everything clean, dry and spotless.

NATURE'S FREEBIE: For any keepers of hens, rather than feed them poultry grit, which is often crushed limestone, oyster or mussel shells, which is mostly calcium and helps them produce hard shells on their eggs, use Mother Nature's own recycling system. Keep your eggshell halves, wash them, dry outside, then break into a fine crumb. Your hens will much prefer eating these that have exactly the right balance of calcium needed for strong egg production. It's less waste in your kitchen, too – your chickens will thank you with plenty of delicious and nutritious eggs.

Laundry fabric softener

This is for those people (and I was one) who used proprietary fabric softeners over many years and had become 'conditioned' (excuse the pun) into believing that clean laundry needed to smell of strong perfume. However, once I read the reverse labels and saw that certain brands increased flammability in clothing, the list of synthetic chemicals was alarming, there was the cost, the single-use, large, coloured plastic bottles and the mouldy mess it made of my washing machine detergent dispenser. I knew I needed to change.

Many of my readers and followers have switched to using this natural product, too, particularly those in hard-water areas who enjoy a cleaner machine. My fabric softener prevents limescale buildup, dissolves soap scum, softens the rinse water and therefore the laundry, and can help to eliminate static cling. There have been a number of people, though, who miss the perfume – they like a pleasing scent to their clean laundry as it is taken from the machine.

For me, the fresh, clean smell from outdoor air drying is the best, though I agree this isn't possible for everyone and there are, of course, the wet, cold winter days when outdoor drying is not possible – a spot of scent doesn't go amiss!

I have tweaked this recipe by adding eucalyptus essential oil and Magic Mixer (see page 14). The eucalyptus oil was a chance discovery. I had a bottle left and found the smell too pungent, so thought I would use it up and begin adding it to my fabric softener. The result was actually very pleasing and surprised me. Eucalyptus has never been my perfume of choice, but it is now for fabric softener. It gives a long-lasting, fresh perfume to my laundry that does not really resemble that strong and pungent eucalyptus scent.

As for the Magic Mixer, my reason for this addition is, as we know, because oil floats on liquids (in this recipe, vinegar and glycerine) and even though the bottle got a shake before use to help disperse the oil, it didn't truly emulsify. Adding Magic Mixer helps the oil to disperse fully, resulting in an even distribution of the perfume, which ensures same dose and effect in every wash cycle.

You will need

glass bottle with a screwtop lid

500ml (17fl oz) white vinegar
30ml (1fl oz) vegetable glycerine
5 drops of eucalyptus essential oil (adjust to suit your preference)
Magic Mixer (5 drops polysorbate 80 or smallest drizzle of honey or glucose)

Add all the ingredients to the bottle and shake to fully mix. I use 2–3 tablespoons in the fabric conditioner compartment of the washing machine drawer.

Washing machine FAQs

Can vinegar harm my washing machine's parts?

My response to this is that 2–3 tablespoons used in the final rinse cycle of around 80 litres (17½ gallons) for a front loader and a huge 150 litres (33 gallons) in a top loader is unlikely to create a significant problem. My machine must be getting on for 10 years old, and it has been enjoying my vinegar-based softener for much of that time. The lifespan of a machine is said to be 7–15 years, depending on use and brand, etc. I firmly believe that the use of washing soda as a water softener in every cycle, my vinegar-based fabric softener and periodic cleaning all contribute to keeping my machine free of limescale, soap scum and odours. My cynical self will say, of course they will not encourage us to make our own for a few pennies when we can be persuaded to buy something more expensive and profit-making for the large companies. I don't actually believe that anyone is worried about the health of our washing machine.

Are essential oils bad for the environment?

Some brands do in fact say that essential oils are harmful to aquatic life, though my understanding is that this is due mainly to the impact of large quantities being disposed of and entering the waterways. In addition, some of the manufacturing and farming methods are not sustainable. There is good news to be had; it is possible to buy organic and/or pesticide- and herbicide-free oils that do not damage plant species survival. For me, I am starting to think about how and where I use the oils and in what quantities. I no longer find them necessary in many recipes – I have managed to wean myself off the need for scent or use instead infused vinegar (see page 181). Essential oils, I guess, are here to stay and can be a more natural solution, being used widely for common discomforts and ailments rather than traditional chemical and pharmaceutical cures.

For green cleaning they bridge a gap, helping the transition from the heavily perfumed, synthetic chemical products to actually needing no perfume at all. I use them sparingly and choose wisely from reputable sources.

Liquid laundry detergent

Laundry is often one of the first 'green' switches – it was for me, and when we see the huge range of 'eco-friendly' laundry products on the market it probably is for many others too. Inevitably they are packaged in a single-use plastic bottle or pouch and usually carry a hefty price tag. We can make our own for an absolute fraction of the price and I know many readers who already make this will never go back. Reuse any 1 litre (34fl oz) bottles that you have. I use orange juice bottles, labels removed, and they have been in circulation now for years.

A similar recipe of mine suggested using soap slivers or single-use soaps, yet the feedback was that some soaps didn't thicken while others were so thick they wouldn't leave the bottle.

I realize now that there are various ingredients added to soap that led to the inconsistent results. I use Marseille unperfumed soap flakes or bars in the recipe below, which should give consistent results.

Use essential oil for perfume, if you prefer, but I don't bother, choosing to use it instead for a lasting fragrance in my fabric softener.

You will need

large knife (if using block soap) or a grater
chopping board
large saucepan or heatproof bowl
measuring jug

spatula or wooden spoon
hand blender
5 x 1 litre (34fl oz) plastic bottles
funnel

150g (5½oz) Marseille unperfumed soap bar or flakes
1 litre (34fl oz) just-boiled water
150g (5½oz) washing soda crystals
20ml (¾fl oz) unperfumed eco-friendly washing-up liquid
2.6 litres (4½ pints) cold water

Using the knife and board or the grater, cut the soap into the smallest pieces possible, then add them to the large pan or bowl. If you have soap flakes this step can be omitted – just add the measure of flakes to the pan. Pour over the just-boiled water. Stir well to combine and dissolve – there may be a few lumps, but no worries as they will be blitzed out later.

Add the washing soda crystals and washing-up liquid and stir through. Use the hand blender to blitz to a smooth cream, then begin to add the cold water, 1 litre (34fl oz) at a time, blitzing between each addition. The detergent will be thick, though still a pouring consistency.

Pour the mixture into the bottles using the funnel, until each of the bottles is three-quarters full. Allow some head space, because it will probably thicken even further once it has gone completely cold and has been standing for a day or two. If you return to your bottles and the detergent seems almost solid, simply give it a good shake to loosen, add water to fill to the top, give it another good shake and it will be fine from now on.

To use, measure 100ml (3½fl oz) per load into a plastic cup and put it straight into the drum. Select a long, eco-friendly, 20°C cycle for optimal cleaning and energy efficiency. What about bacteria, you may ask? I have had many questions about bacteria, and one in particular that I remember was from a very worried follower because they had been warned about a concern regarding bacteria on socks. What is the world coming to? Socks worn for a normal day will surely be fine with a 20°C eco wash. Sports kit or very smelly or muddy socks will need a washing soda (naturally anti-bac) pre-soak. My personal opinion is that we have become brainwashed into believing that all bacteria is bad, when in fact it is essential to health. It lives on our skin and in our gut, and by attempting to wipe it out altogether by using chemical additives it can create other problems along the line. I may be a lone voice here, but I will not be convinced otherwise.

Wool/delicates detergent

When the 'green living' addiction really takes hold, as it has done with me, I consider the 'end of life' of most items that I buy, and that has to include clothes. I understand that everything we buy leaves a footprint of some kind, but for me the question to consider is how deep is that footprint?

When it came to clothing I was very guilty of not disposing of it in an environmentally friendly way, and when I look at the hasty, inexpensive purchases that I have made over the years that will have ended up in landfill, I shudder knowing that, however long ago that may have been, they will still very likely be there. Unlike cotton, linen, wool and silk, which are compostable, my polyester, nylon and other man-made fabrics will still be on this Earth somewhere. I read that estimates suggest polyester will take up to 200 years to decompose. I now always consider what will happen to items when I am finished with them and what 'throwing them away' really means. Nothing is truly thrown away – it is still on our planet somewhere, having been buried, dumped or incinerated into hazardous ash.

I try, where possible, to invest in woollens rather than polyester alternatives when it comes to jumpers, and I have a number of woollen hand knits that I adore. Just as an aside, I have returned to knitting in the evenings using 100 per cent recycled cotton. I am expecting it will not pill and bobble as wool often does. This has a couple of lifestyle advantages for me; as well as producing a home-made piece of clothing, it also prevents me from 'double screening' with one eye on the TV and one on my phone. I can knit and watch the TV, but the phone is put on charge and not picked up until the next day.

Woollens are expensive, and even using a machine's woollens cycle I have had some not-too-pleasing results. Detergents can also be a little harsh, even my home-made and eco-friendly recipes contain washing soda, which may weaken fibres by causing them to shrink or felt. Washing soda is fine on cotton.

Natural, unscented soap flakes are perfect for use when washing woollens, yet I struggled to get them to fully dissolve. Even after washing I could detect residual soap, I could feel it, an almost sticky waxy texture, and I could sometimes see it – especially on dark-coloured clothes. There could be tiny white specks or marks where undissolved soap had remained lodged amongst the woollen fibres. I decided to make a thick, cream woollens detergent that would readily mix in tepid water. Here then is my recipe and care guide for home knits and expensive woollens.

You will need

grater
small bowl
weighing scales
large heatproof jug or bowl
spatula
stick blender
500ml (17fl oz) glass jar with a screwtop lid

50g (1¾oz) soap flakes or natural soap bar
300ml (10fl oz) just-boiled water
25ml (1fl oz) vegetable glycerine
a few drops of essential oil (optional, I like honeysuckle or white linen)

Measure the flakes or grate the soap bar into the small bowl. Place an empty bowl or jug onto the scales and set to zero. Pour over the just-boiled water, then add 1 tablespoon of soap at a time, stirring to dissolve. The soap flakes will probably dissolve readily, but if they settle into clumps the stick blender is called for to assist with the mixing. Once a smooth creamy liquid is achieved, stir through the glycerine and essential oil (if using), then pour into the glass jar to store.

I have a plastic measuring spoon that I keep in the jar for scooping it out when needed. The gentle detergent cream keeps for at least 6 months in the sealed jar.

To use

I always hand-wash woollens. Add 1 tablespoon of the detergent to a large washing-up bowl, pour over tepid water and swish around using your hand until the cream is dispersed. For more than one jumper you may need to use the sink, so double up on the detergent and water.

Turn the jumper inside out, fold into 4 (in half widthways and then in half lengthways), then gently submerge it into the solution. I then leave my woollens for several hours to soak, and I have found this will dissolve any light stains and grubbiness.

After this time, gently agitate the woollen garment, squeezing here and there. No rubbing, pushing, pulling or wringing the item, as this can damage the fibres.

Lift the heavily soaked woollen from the washing water with no wringing, just a gentle squeeze to remove excess water. Then add 1–2 tablespoons of my fabric softener (see page 200) to a bowl of tepid water and gently rinse the woollen – again, no rough handling, a gentle swish around in the water is enough.

Historically, woollens would be rolled in towels to absorb excess moisture, then dried flat. I still do this with very precious items, though I have found instead that briefly using the washing machine saves on having to then dry soaking-wet towels as well as the jumper. I place my sodden, rinsed woollens into the drum of the machine and select a spin cycle.

My spin cycle is 12 minutes, but that is far too long and excess spinning can felt and shrink woollens. Instead, I stand over the machine – if the phone rings, I ignore it, if someone comes to the door, tough. My jumper has all of my attention. My machine will take 2–3 minutes, gently turning and draining excess moisture from the jumpers. At 8 minutes remaining it will begin to spin – slowly to start with. I allow this spin for only 1–2 minutes, depending on how many woollens are in there – a few rotations of the drum. I then turn the machine off.

There may be machines out there that don't co-operate with this method and will lock until the cycle is complete, though I have always found that turning the power off will release any locking. If this method doesn't work for you, pop the sodden woollens into the drum and allow the machine to 'drain' excess water without the spin.

This gentle spin action is sufficient to remove excess water without subjecting the garments to undue force. I then remove the jumper, lay it out flat, gently reshape it and dry it flat, or lay it over my drying rack. I don't iron woollens.

For woollens that are light in colour and maybe stained around the neck or cuffs, a pre-treatment may be necessary. Use a spray of water to dampen the stained areas, then rub it into the stain using a blob of cream cleaner (see page 11) – massage this in then pop the jumper in a plastic bag for a few hours so it doesn't dry out. This treatment will loosen any stubborn stains, particularly makeup, grease or oil. After this pre-treatment, wash as described above.

> **TIP:** Many lovers of sewing and embroidery will probably already know this, but a slip of the hand when sewing and a prick from a needle can have catastrophic effects. I made a christening gown for each of my grand-daughters and I remember setting in the tiniest sleeve into the body of this very small gown, only to then prick my finger and get a small blood spot on the white satin fabric. Rather than panic, I wet a small piece of the same spare fabric using my own saliva and dabbed at the spot, and it instantly lifted.

Conker detergent mark II

I adore Mother Nature's free offerings and saponins contained in conkers and English ivy really work. Detergents are effective because they reduce water surface tension, allowing the cleaner to emulsify in the water, removing stains and dirt from laundry during agitation, suspending them in the water then washing out in the rinse. Saponins (nature's own bubbly detergent) does exactly the same thing without polluting our waterways. The more you know, the more there is to know! I discovered the wonder of saponins in conkers some years ago and set out to make my own detergent using them, which I documented in my first book, *Clean & Green*. Since then, I have made a number of discoveries, so I consider it worth revisiting for a few extra tips for those who want to make this natural, free, laundry detergent in a way that is more pleasing to the eye, less faff and just as much fun. Children love to collect conkers in the autumn, so gathering shiny, large conkers is a job they will do without having to be asked twice. Once home, pack the conkers into boxes or bags of 130g (4¼oz – about 10), label and freeze, and this quantity will make 1 litre (34fl oz). Alternatively, freeze them all in one box and use between 10 and 12 for each litre (34fl oz).

Freezing the conkers before using has two advantages. Firstly, once thawed the hard, shiny shell easily peels off, leaving the pale, creamy coloured seed, which contains the saponins. It is not possible to do this to a fresh conker, as the shell remains stuck to the fleshy inside. Secondly, by not using the dark brown outer shell the finished bottle of detergent has a pleasing colour – very pale cream rather than a coffee brown, which is the result if the shells are left intact.

You will need

large sharp knife
wooden cutting board
1 litre (34fl oz) heatproof measuring jug

wooden spoon
very fine tea strainer or small sieve
1 litre (34fl oz) bottle with a screwtop lid (maybe a used detergent bottle)
funnel
hand-held blender

130g (4¼oz) shiny ripe horse chestnuts (about 10 conkers/buckeyes)
1 litre (34fl oz) just-boiled water
5–10 drops of essential oil (optional)
Magic Mixer (5 drops polysorbate 80 or smallest drizzle of honey or glucose) (optional, see page 14)

Thaw the conkers for a few hours, then slice each one into 2. Peel off the shiny shells and add these to the compost. Slice each half of pale cream flesh into several pieces, the smaller the better, and add to the jug. Pour over 500ml (18fl oz) of the just-boiled water, stir with the wooden spoon then leave to infuse for 8 hours or overnight.

The next day, use the tea strainer to strain the creamy coloured liquid into the bottle, using the funnel to catch any drips. The remaining conker pieces in the jug will have softened overnight, so use the hand-held blender to blitz them to a thick puree. Pour over then the remaining just-boiled water, stir, then leave for 2–3 hours. You will see many foaming bubbles from this second batch. Again, with the funnel in the bottle, strain the second batch into the bottle that contains the first 500ml (17fl oz).

Add 5–10 drops of essential oil for perfume, if using, and Magic Mixer (5 drops polysorbate 80 or smallest drizzle of honey or glucose) to ensure emulsification and the same dose of perfume for every use. Give the bottle a shake and it is ready to use. Compost the pulp.

To use

Measure 50ml (1¾fl oz) into a cup or bottle lid and pop it straight into the washing machine drum with the clothes along with 2 tablespoons of washing soda (to soften the water) into the detergent drawer.

> **NOTES:** Conker detergent doesn't have a long shelf life. After a couple of weeks, especially when kept in a warm place, it will begin to ferment and fizz when the bottle is opened. For best results, freeze whole conkers then make 1 litre (34fl oz) of the detergent as and when required. Conkers themselves do not keep fresh and juicy for a long time, and once dried out will become hard and not give the best-quality detergent, which is why it is best to freeze them as soon as you get them home.

Magic suds – ivy detergent

After discovering the wonder of natural detergent saponins found in ivy leaves and conkers and first documenting this in *Clean & Green*, I realized that although this was fun, free and wondrous – it was also slightly inconvenient. Did I really want to be running outside with my scissors to harvest fresh ivy leaves every time I needed to put the washer on?

But now you can make a handy litre of liquid detergent quickly, easily and it does the job.

You will need

Scissors
Large saucepan and lid
Sieve, tea strainer and funnel
Jug
1 litre (34fl oz) bottle
100g English ivy leaves
1.1 litres (37fl oz) cold water

English ivy is available all year round and I have a supply that I leave to grow freely in a wild corner of my garden. Choose large, old leaves with visible veins – there lie the natural saponins that, once released, will do a great laundry job.

Wash the leaves in cold water (you will be amazed at the dust they collect!) then, using the scissors, snip the leaves into large strips and place them into the saucepan. Add 1.1 litres of cold water.

Bring the pan to the boil, reduce the heat then simmer for 20 minutes with a lid on. Turn off the heat and leave to infuse and go completely cold.

Once cold, pass through a sieve into the jug, squeeze out the leaves and pop the leaves onto the compost heap.

The minty green liquid has a pleasing pine type fragrance so I don't add any essential oils.

Pour from the jug through a tea strainer and into the 1 litre bottle – you will see the suds forming already.

To use

The first time I made this and before using I had to think about dosage. I considered the detergent to look watery and thin so decided to pour 150ml into a measuring cup and into the drum of the machine. I chose my normal long 20°C eco wash cycle, 2 tablespoons of washing soda in the detergent compartment, my own fabric softener along with a collection of grubby towels and cloths.

Twenty minutes into the wash cycle I could see suds were forming – this was great. Forty minutes in and those suds had doubled until one hour into the wash cycle the glass door of the washing machine was a mass of white thick suds. I realised Mother Nature had excelled on this occasion and I had underestimated the power of the watery detergent.

With this in mind may I suggest the following:

50ml (1¾fl oz) magic suds detergent (100ml (3½fl oz) if your items are heavily soiled)

2 tbsp washing soda in the detergent drawer (I use it to soften water, help with the cleaning and prevent limescale build-up as I live in a very hard water area)

2 tbsp fabric softener (see page 200)

20°C cold long eco wash cycle (mine is 2 hours 18 minutes and uses less than a third of the energy of a 40°C cycle).

I am delighted with this detergent – but as with conker detergent, and being totally natural, it has only a short shelf life of 2-3 weeks, after which time it will start to fizz and ferment especially in a warm kitchen or during warm weather.

My yellow woollen coat – I washed it!

I have a bright, sunshine-yellow, full-length woollen coat – and I adore it. It doesn't get worn often, even though I have had it for some years. I save it for dull days or a special outing, especially in winter time. I have had so many smiley comments about my yellow coat – I think bright colours are uplifting, though definitely not that practical.

My last book tour took me up and down the country and I decided that, as it was early spring and the weather forecast was good, I would take along my yellow coat and would wear it with black jeans and a black jumper. Simple, easy-to-wear clothes, yet bright and cheery too.

After a fairly hectic schedule, I remember being on the train home and deciding to take off my coat to place it on the overhead rack, as ever, turning it inside out before doing so, and saw, with absolute shock horror, that the coat was filthy! Once home, on closer inspection I could see that my black jeans had transferred dye not only to the inside of my coat but also to the sleeves, the cuffs and the front.

This coat is 60 per cent wool, the rest being man-made fibres, and is recommended 'dry clean only'. However, I was prepared to experiment with my much-loved yellow coat. I have not used the dry cleaners since 'going green', due to the toxic chemicals involved, and so I have washed many dry-clean-only garments, but never a woollen coat. The fact that I decided to include this story in this book should indicate that this was a complete success.

You will need

2 cloths
wooden spoon

bicarbonate of soda in a sugar shaker
4 tbsp woollen detergent (see page 206)
1–2 tsp green bleach (optional, for light colours only)
4–5 tbsp fabric softener (see page 200)

This method works best done in the bath. I started by laying the coat out on a work surface and dusting the soiled areas with bicarbonate of soda. I find using a sugar shaker results in an even distribution or, if necessary, a little more right where I want it.

After a light sprinkle I went over it with a dry cloth, massaging it into the woollen fibres. With a dampened cloth, I then worked at the very soiled areas, hoping to remove the staining. While I was able to remove much of it, my coat was still looking grubby, which is when I decided to use the bath.

I added the woollen detergent to the bath along with the green bleach, then poured over some hot water and stirred the solution around with a wooden spoon until all was dissolved. I then added enough cold water that the bath was nearly half full and the solution tepid, and it was in with the coat.

Leaving the garment on a plastic hanger (no metal hanger or wooden hanger with metal hook that could leave a rust stain) and buttoned up, I laid it onto the water and left it to sink in and absorb the water in its own time.

After an hour or so the coat had sunk underneath the water – I used the wooden spoon to push out any air holes so that the whole coat was submerged, then I left it overnight.

The next day I let the water out of the bath, leaving the coat as it was. Once the water was gone, it was in with the plug again to half-fill the bath with cold water, adding my fabric softener at the same time.

I allowed the coat to swim in the clean water for 10 minutes or so, then pulled out the plug.

The coat, as you can imagine, was heavy and water soaked, so I lifted it by the hanger, placing a bowl underneath to catch the drips, and took it into the shower to drip dry. Had the weather been fine I would have taken it outside. Once the dripping had stopped, I hung the coat in a warm room to finish drying completely – it took two days!

The result – my coat looked like new, apart from one small area where I had overdone the rubbing with the bicarb, which I think had affected the colour. I think only I would notice, though, but it's something I wouldn't do again.

A few notes: Before deciding to wash a dry-clean-only garment, try to first spot clean it with a pad dipped in surgical spirit – it may save washing the whole item. For dark-coloured clothes, use only the woollen detergent and not the green bleach. My fabric softener is used to dissolve any residual detergent left in the garment. Leaving it to drip dry naturally rather than even the shortest spin will ensure the garment retains its shape, and there is no need to press it afterwards.

I tend to take the risk and wash dry-clean-only garments, but consider the following before you take the plunge:

1. How precious is the garment – could you bear to spoil it?

2. Often, dry cleaning labels are added because the fabric may well be washable but hadn't been pre-shrunk before being made into a garment. In these cases, even the gentlest of washes may shrink the fabric or the lining.

3. If having a go with 100 per cent wool, don't use washing soda as it can affect the dye and/or fibres. Use the gentlest wool detergent recipe above.

4. If you decide to have a go with 100 per cent silk I would start with a one-part vinegar to two-parts tepid water, to avoid any colour runs or damage.

5. Faux suede – just a mention here that a follower asked for my advice for cleaning a faux suede jacket that had a coffee stain down one sleeve. It was dry clean only and the dry cleaners had said it probably couldn't be removed. She was prepared to try anything because the jacket couldn't be worn in it's stained state. A soak in the bath in one part vinegar and two parts tepid water – left to drip dry outside in the shade (not full sun) and the jacket was stain free and back to perfection!

Tea towels

I am an abuser of tea towels and use at least one per day, because although I start off with good intentions I end up using them for all manner of things. As well as drying dishes, though I do have a dishwasher, I will reach for a tea towel to mop up spills, I also use them well-folded in place of oven gloves, and if my dog Wilfred spots one he will take it from the rail and drag it around the floor.

There is no wonder then that my tea towels get into a state, yet I can keep them clean and bright without the need of a very hot 90°C wash cycle, which, apart from using a lot of energy and obvious cost, can also, I have found, fix some stains. Cold washing it is for me.

I save my tea towels and wash them once a week. An overnight pre-soak in washing soda and green bleach will dissolve grease stains, sanitize and loosen stains before a long cold wash. Both green bleach and washing soda are naturally anti-bac, though the soak alone is not sufficient to remove the stains – a long wash cycle is necessary (e.g. not a quick 30-minute cycle). My experience is that cold washing is more effective at dissolving stains than a hot wash.

You will need

TO PRE-SOAK
bucket or large sink
wooden spoon

4 tbsp washing soda
2 tsp green bleach

TO WASH
2 tbsp washing soda
2 tsp green bleach
100ml (3½fl oz) laundry detergent (see page 202)
2–3 tbsp fabric softener (see page 200)

Once I have a collection of tea towels that's sufficient for a load, I will start with an overnight soak. Place the washing soda and green bleach into a bucket or large sink and add enough just-boiled or very hot water to dissolve the powders, stirring with the wooden spoon. The solution will foam. Add sufficient cold water to take the temperature down to tepid (feeling neither hot nor cold), then add the tea towels, press down to submerge in the water with the wooden spoon and leave overnight.

The next day, wring out each tea towel by hand then place them into the drum of the washing machine. Take a look at the colour of the soaking water and see just how effective an overnight soak can be. This solution can go down the sink, knowing there is no harm being done to our waterways.

Add the detergent straight into the drum, then add the washing soda and green bleach to the detergent dispenser and my fabric softener to the softener compartment.

I choose a long cold 20°C cycle, and mine has a duration of over 2 hours. Don't be alarmed – this cycle uses a third of the energy and the same amount of water as a 40°C cycle. Around 90 per cent of the energy used by the washing machine is to heat the water, as the simple turning of the drum to move and agitate the laundry uses very little energy. After the wash, air dry outside and your tea towels will be beautifully clean.

I am often asked why I add the detergent directly into the drum and not into the dispenser. The reason for that is, for me, living in a very hard water area, I need to use washing soda as a water softener with each wash cycle. Not only does it work hard on stains by softening the water, it also prevents limescale build-up, which would otherwise damage my machine.

If I then add liquid detergent to the dry washing soda in the dispenser, the soda crystals could clump together and may not then find their way into the drum to wash the laundry. Separating the two ensures I am not left with a sludgy residue in the detergent drawer after the wash cycle.

I use this recipe and method for tea towels for many other badly stained items as well as items with odours (muddy sports kit and gym kits).

CLOTHING AND LAUNDRY CARE

Hand-knitted dishcloths

You can buy recycled cotton for dishcloths – an off-white colour – and I have to say a hand-knitted dishcloth is robust and effective. Cast on 40 stitches using 4mm (US6) needles, Work in rows of garter stitch, (or play around with stitch patterns if you are an experienced knitter) for about 40 rows or until you achieve about a 23cm (9 in) square cloth. Cast off, and you have a very hardwearing, robust dishcloth and a great little gift idea for the newbie greenie.

I was sent a hand-knitted cotton dishcloth by a follower during Covid as a thank you for my daily posts, which she said kept her going. Many years on and this dishcloth is still in use. It will stand any number of green bleach and boiling water soaks, wrings out to nearly dry and has kept its shape. Measuring 30cm x 20cm (12in x 8in) and made with a simple stocking stitch, my way forward is hand-knitted. I like different colours for different jobs: pink for the sink and blue for the loo! If you're not a knitter, have a look at the fabrics in your house. Upcycling old bedding, towels and cotton t-shirts into cleaning and polishing cloths was something my grandmother used to do, and did I ever think I would do the same? Not at all. I used to regularly pick up a pack of microfibre cleaning cloths that I used until they looked unsightly then tossed them into the bin, not even thinking I was leaching plastics into the waterways and adding to the enormous landfill and plastics problem.

I now take pride in my cleaning cloths – the used ones are saved up then have a weekly soak in washing soda and green bleach followed by a machine wash, before blowing with pride on the washing line, clean and bright.

Dye from jeans onto trainers

New jeans and new trainers – so many cries for help, because the first time on, the dye from the jeans has rubbed onto the new suede trainers or canvas shoes. The main advice is not to wet anything! Leather trainers can be wiped using a damp cloth dipped in cream cleaner (see page 11).

You will need

> cloth
> suede brush (for suede)
> stiff brush, smooth pumice stone or clean pencil rubber (for suede)
>
> bicarbonate of soda (in a bowl or a sugar shaker)

Sprinkle the bicarbonate of soda over the shoe then use a lightly dampened cloth to gently work at the stained areas of suede or canvas. The light abrasion and bicarb's natural cleaning powers will lift the dye without damaging or leaving a water mark on the material.

Gently brush with a suede brush, or if you don't have one a smooth pumice stone or clean (not blackened) pencil rubber. Canvas shoes should be brushed using a stiff brush – a metal suede brush may be too harsh.

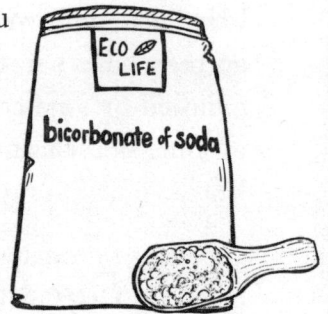

Avoid pilling of jumpers

How many times have even your very expensive jumpers and hand knits suffered pilling – those little fuzzy bobbles of wool that appear particularly on the underside of sleeves and under the arms of jumpers? I have spent so much time on finding out what causes them, how to avoid them and what to do to treat them.

Prevention

My experience, confirmed by further reading, suggests that pilling is reduced significantly when woollens are washed less and not every time they are worn. I have a cable Arran hand knit, which is a very thick, gorgeous jumper that I knitted over ten years ago. It has never been washed. It is worn on the coldest of days with several layers underneath and is as lovely now as it was the day I finished it. No pilling or bobbling.

There is a tendency, I think, to over-launder our clothing, including woollens. Wash the garments only when necessary – too much laundering will weaken the fibres and shorten the life of the garment. Rather than regularly washing your much-loved garments, give them a refresh by hanging them outside to take in some air, or if the weather doesn't permit, try using my Easy Breeze fabric spray, see page 234.

Woollens I now always wash by hand without the agitation of the machine. Detergent, too, plays an important part. Before going green, I used whatever detergent was at hand, and of course they always promised to be kind to delicates. I now understand that they may not have been kind at all. I now wash woollen garments using my own delicates/woollens detergent (see page 206). Wash woollen garments inside out to protect the right side of the garment and simply lay the jumper in the solution with very little disturbance (see woollens washing on page 206). Tumble dryers too can contribute to pilling, felting and shrinkage of woollens. I prefer to dry mine flat either outside or inside, laying them loosely over a ceiling rack or drying rack on a towel so that ridges are not left on the garment.

It goes to say that woollens will mostly be worn when the weather is on the chilly side, but be careful when layering up. I had a corduroy-type waistcoat that I wore over a favourite jumper, only to discover that due to the friction of the two materials the jumper came off much worse. The corduroy rubbing against the inside sleeve of my sweater caused me a huge pilling problem. Car seat belts, too, can create similar friction that jumpers hate.

Treatment and prevention

There are pilling removal gadgets available that will shave and remove the annoying fuzzy bobbles, and I understand they are effective though I have never bought one. I choose instead to gently cut away any offending fuzz without pulling and tugging and weakening any other fibres.

I used to believe that a pilling was due to the poor quality of the wool, but this isn't the case – even the most expensive woollen jumper can suffer. It's actually the result of fibres loosening on the surface of fabric and then twisting together into tiny clumps. Those clumps gather lint and dust, often making them look darker in colour than the garment.

I have read that placing a brand-new jumper in a plastic bag and into the freezer for 48 hours before the first wearing or washing can prevent pilling. I have tried this on a new jumper and at the time of writing – so far so good!

Prevent and take action against clothes moths

It is bad enough when a favourite jumper suffers a shrink, or it develops a few fuzzy bobbles – those can be quickly sorted and minimized in the future. However, the dreaded clothes moths are silent destructors of natural fibres, whether they be wool, silk, cashmere or fur and, I have read, they're not averse to the odd linen and cotton snack.

Please don't ever think they won't find you. Their most active times are during the spring and summer months, and then again in early autumn, but they can be a problem all the year round in warmer homes. I have yet to spot an adult moth – they are nocturnal so they are busy while I am sleeping, but sadly I have known to my cost that they have been present because there has been damage, in the form of tiny holes on my much-loved clothing.

Just as an aside, the moth itself doesn't do the chewing, it is the tiny grubs as they hatch from the eggs laid by the adult moth that create havoc amongst the soft, warm woollens.

Clothes and carpet moths love dark, warm conditions, hate to be disturbed and need a few natural jumpers to get nestled into, where they will lay their eggs knowing they have a ready food supply to feed their young on later when the grubs hatch.

Unfortunately, often it is not until we have a problem that we ask the questions, and that has been my experience. I reached for my favourite, fine-knit, 100 per cent woollen sweater to find it peppered with tiny holes. No sign of moths, they had long gone, as had the grubs that had obviously fattened themselves, matured and flown off too. I was furious – why had they just picked on this one jumper? Clearly because it was the only 100 per cent natural garment in the drawer.

Treatment

There are products on the market that promise to eradicate clothes and carpet moths. I picked one such packet off the shelf and read the long list of chemicals – especially the statement: 'very toxic to aquatic life'. Toxic to aquatic life probably means it is also toxic to humans.

To treat your clothes, the whole wardrobe or chest of drawers needs to be cleared out and the clothes placed into a bag and put into the freezer for at least 48 hours. After that they should be washed and air-dried if possible. Dust the empty drawers, cupboards and wardrobe with diatomaceous earth (see page 198), and leave it on for 24–48 hours before vacuuming off. Diatomaceous earth causes insects to dry out and die by absorbing the oils and fats from them, and it will remain active for as long as it is kept dry.

Prevention

This is by far the easiest and most effective way to avoid clothes moths. Store your favourite natural-fibre jumpers, etc., in sealed containers such as boxes or bags that moths cannot enter. Use repellents such as lavender bags, lavender wands (see below), cedar balls or my Easy Breeze fabric spray – see recipe on page 235.

For carpet moths, vacuum regularly, keep the room well aired and sprinkle over an occasional dusting of diatomaceous earth in a sugar shaker (perfumed with a few drops of lavender oil), and leave it on the carpet for a few days.

I have a friend whose wife sadly went into a residential home. The household cleaning routine lapsed, unfortunately, and when he did finally get around to moving the sofa to vacuum underneath, the precious silk carpet square that had been treasured over their married life had been destroyed by moths.

The trick is to keep the silent vandals at bay – using a few simple, yet effective, natural prevention methods rather than having to resort to toxic chemical sprays and solutions and lots of work.

Lavender wand

I grow lavender, and as well as giving me a wonderful show in early summer, it provides so many useful additional benefits.

I spotted a lavender wand smartly put together in a small gift shop on holiday. It was so beautiful and practical, plus a fantastic yet useful gift idea, so I decided to make them myself. I have gifted so many of these and once you have explained the many uses, they will bring a smile to even the most difficult people to buy for.

Hang these by the loop around coat hangers in the wardrobe to perfume clothing and deter moths from woollen coats, suits and jumpers, or lay them in drawers for the same effect. A bunch displayed upright in a jar or vase make a beautiful dried-flower display, while also adding subtle natural perfume to the room.

In time the natural perfume from the wand will fade, so I then give mine a livener by adding a few drops of lavender essential oil. I have read that lavender essential oil is safe around cats.

This is a pleasing pastime to do outside when the sun is shining, and the method below will make one wand, so scale up if you are making these for gifts from your harvest.

You will need

> 17 stems of lavender flowers complete with a 30cm (12in) stem (I choose faded flowers, still lots of perfume but the bees have finished with them)
> 1m (3ft) length of 5mm (¼in) wide ribbon
> 5mm–2.5cm (½–1in) thick ribbon, for the bow and hanging loop
> scissors

The first wand will probably be a little slack or not quite perfect (mine was), but you will soon get the hang of it. The secret to success is to keep the wand ribbon as tight and as snug as you can and don't rush.

Take the bunch of long-stemmed blooms and hold them by the fist of one hand, holding them in such a way that the flower heads are above the hand and the long stalks below. Use the free hand to remove any straggly leaves. Then, taking the length of ribbon, tie it into a double knot around the top of the bunch, where the hand is, securing it directly under the neck of the flowers. The bunch of lavender is now in one piece.

Turn the bunch upside down, take the tight cluster of blooms and hold gently in the palm of one hand. The collection of stalks will be uppermost. Make sure the length of ribbon is free. Use the other hand then to one by one fold the long stalks down and over the blooms, collecting each one as it comes down and clasping it by the hand holding the blooms.

Evenly place each stalk as it is folded down over the collection of blooms until by the end of the task a cage of stalks is formed around the buds and already you can see the start of a wand.

CLOTHING AND LAUNDRY CARE • 233

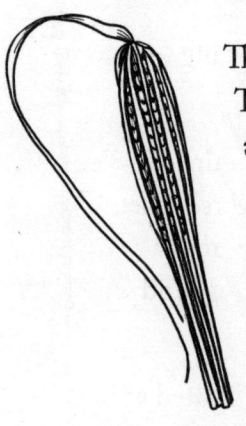

This next bit can be tricky until you get going. Take the long length of ribbon, which is loose and hanging at the top of the wand, and weave it under and over the stalks around the flowers to keep them in place. Starting feels clumsy and it is necessary to lift alternate stalks in order to be able to weave successfully. As work continues down the wand it gets easier and the hands get clever at tightening and weaving at the same time.

The efficient wand will be tight and secure, the flower buds inside the cage cannot be seen, yet the natural lavender fragrance will permeate the whole wand. Tie off the ribbon at the base of the wand to secure the weaving.

Use the scissors to trim the stalks to an even length, then take the second length of ribbon to form a decorative bow and hanging loop, if required.

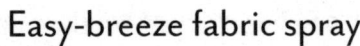

Easy-breeze fabric spray

There are many sprays on the market that promise to freshen clothing, add a pleasing scent to rooms, upholstery and curtains. The 'natural', eco-friendly brands often come with a hefty price tag, not to mention the pretty packaging and sometimes an aerosol can.

The non-eco-friendly versions unfortunately contained our now-recognizable statement in small type on the reverse label: 'toxic to aquatic life with long-lasting effects'. Do I really want to be spraying synthetic chemicals on my clothing and around my house?

I decided to make my own, and am absolutely delighted with this easy recipe. I spent some time developing a subtly scented natural spray after seeing those available to buy. I love this easy recipe that is mixed at home and eco-friendly, and I use it regularly to freshen clothing, add a pleasing scent to rooms, upholstery and curtains. This recipe has one additional benefit, in that it is a natural moth deterrent.

You will need

500ml (17fl oz) jar with a screwtop lid
300ml (10fl oz) spray bottle
small funnel

250ml (8fl oz) cheap vodka or odourless surgical spirit (available to buy or infuse your own using citrus peel, see page 182)
20 drops of essential oil that will repel moths (lavender, rosemary, lemon, bergamot, sage, peppermint)
Magic Mixer (10 drops polysorbate 80 or 1 drop honey or glucose) (see page 14)

CLOTHING AND LAUNDRY CARE • 235

Pour the measured vodka or odourless surgical spirit into the jar, add the essential oil of choice followed by the Magic Mixer, which will effectively emulsify the vodka and oil, ensuring even perfume in every spray and no oily residue. Secure the screwtop lid and give a good shake. Use the funnel to then transfer to the spray bottle and it is ready to use. A fine mist onto woollen clothing will repel moths.

As a clothes, upholstery, room and odour spray

I have huge concerns about air-freshening products that can be purchased for use around the home. I routinely download product safety data sheets – some can be as long as 16 pages – and they can make interesting reading.

I read one such sheet that warned that if fabric freshener was inhaled and the breathing affected you should seek medical advice. Really!? It is inevitable that a clothes spray will be inhaled. Also, as an aside, there is further data that states 'do not dispose of in the sewer'.

I shudder when I see television advertisements spraying aerosols of 'this and that', promising spring freshness to rooms, toilets and bathrooms. There are even those that are plugged into the mains, ensuring the chemical pollutants are regularly topped up. I have even seen sprays on the market that are directed straight onto a pillow and promising a good night's sleep – oh my word! Then on examination of the safety data sheet, there is a warning that states 'may cause itching, rashes and hives' and to consult a physician.

Marketing is so powerful. We are being encouraged and brainwashed into spending money to harm ourselves. Can we just open a window to freshen the air and come off our devices in the evening to help with sleep?

I do not use air, clothes and room fresheners extensively, but there are times when a quick squirt will help to freshen a room or neutralize odours on dry-clean-only clothing. There may be a thick jumper that maybe smells a bit fusty or has taken on cooking smells. It doesn't need a wash – just a freshen up. Thanks to this simple recipe there is no need to reach for the harmful chemical alternatives.

For room odours, cooking smells, clothing odours, shoes, etc.

Mix the ingredients in the jar as above and choose your essential oil, then transfer to a spray bottle – I like white linen for clothing and lemon for cooking smells, etc. If you don't want to use any perfume, leave it out. Though I have to say I do prefer a pleasing scent.

Vodka quickly evaporates and will help to neutralize odours, particularly those of smoke and mildew, by killing odour-causing bacteria. The alcohol in vodka works as a natural deodorizer and neutralizes unpleasant smells.

I remember one follower messaged me gleefully stating that a child had vomited in the car, and while the clean-up was successful a lingering odour had remained. However, she used my Easy Breeze fabric spray with lavender and the problem was quickly resolved.

Try a spray on smelly trainers and shoes, clothing and furniture that has taken on the aroma of tobacco smoke, or a dry-clean-only piece of clothing that has a lingering faint whiff of body odour. A spray after cooking will help to neutralize residual kitchen smells and a small bottle kept in the bathroom can be handy!

Nature's freebie: perfumed distilled ironing water

Those that use a steam iron and live in a hard-water area will know that unless distilled water is used in the water chamber limescale will build up inside, causing unsightly brown marks to splutter out onto laundry, and it will affect the performance of your iron and shorten its life.

Plastic bottles of distilled ironing water containing a range of synthetic perfumes promising summer breeze scents and wild-flower meadows are available to buy, but why bother when Mother Nature has her own distilled water and natural scents for free – without the plastic packaging!

Rainwater is Mother Nature's free distilled water, and this can be perfumed using a range of natural scents.

You will need

1 litre (34fl oz) jug
saucepan

fine sieve
funnel
1 litre (34fl oz) bottle

natural scents – a slice of lemon, orange or grapefruit zest, fresh lavender flowers, rose petals, rosemary or mint sprigs

Start by gathering your fresh rainwater. I am excited when the heavens open, the rain bounces off the paths and pavements and is thundering down the downpipe. I run out with my jug and pop it under the spout of the drainpipe from the greenhouse roof, and it fills in seconds. If you have a rainwater butt and the water is clean, that is fine, though if it is green and smelly, leave that for the garden. There are many ingenious ways of collecting rainwater – even a large pan put outside during a rainstorm will probably give you enough to make your own ironing water.

Place 1 litre (34fl oz) of rainwater into a saucepan and add your scent of choice. During summer a handful of lavender flowers will infuse the water beautifully, but even when flower scents are not in season slices of lemon, orange or grapefruit can be used or add a few spent lemons after using the rind and juice for something else rather than use a whole fruit.

Bring the water to the boil then turn off the heat, add a lid and leave it to go completely cold. Strain through the fine sieve back into a clean jug. This will remove any debris, flowers and fruit bits – and what remains is your own natural distilled ironing water, which will not scale up your iron.

The chamber of a steam iron usually holds around 250ml (9fl oz), but unless I have lots of ironing to do I fill to about half-full then discard into a jug after the ironing session (to add back to the bottle once cold).

I don't leave water in the iron – manufacturers usually recommend that the water tank is emptied after use and the iron stored in an upright position, as this avoids corrosion and damage to the soleplate.

This ironing water doesn't contain any anti-fungal or preserving properties, so I would not expect it to keep on the shelf for longer than about a month.

TIP: Those who use a condenser tumble dryer will have their own distilled water in the condenser chamber – don't waste it.

Fusty-smelling towels or clothing

Ever had the problem of fusty-smelling clothing, towels or bedding, and even after a wash the odour is still there? It is that fusty dank odour that comes from a wet dishcloth or face flannel that has been scrunched up and left in a ball by the sink. It may be a damp towel that has been left in a heap on the bathroom floor – not necessarily a lazy action, it may have fallen from the towel rack. Then there is the sweaty, damp sports kit that has been left in the sports bag in the car and not remembered until the day before it is needed for training – that's family life, in my experience.

The odour occurs because the damp items are starting to grow mildew or mould. Mould will thrive in warm damp conditions, the spores are in the air anyway and a damp towel, flannel or piece of clothing will soon take on that musty smell even though there may not be anything visible going on. Washing alone and dousing in lots of false perfumes may not remove the odour, but a natural washing-soda soak will. Washing soda is naturally anti-bac and the solution acts as a fungicide that can kill mould and mildew and also neutralize any odours.

You will need

For a large sink full
wooden spoon

5–6 tbsp washing soda
laundry detergent (see page 202)

Add the washing soda to the sink, pour over hot water to cover the sink base and stir using the wooden spoon until the washing soda has dissolved and the solution is cloudy. Then add enough cold water to produce a tepid, deep bath and soak the items.

Use the wooden spoon to poke at the items to ensure that the laundry is well saturated and below the water line. Leave overnight. Next day, squeeze out any excess solution, then wash in the machine.

Choose your favoured detergent and wash cycle. I make my own liquid detergent (see page 204) and I wash everything on a cold, 20°C, long eco cycle, saving energy, protecting the dye and fibres in my clothes, releasing fewer microplastics into the water system, dissolving (rather than fixing) stains, and saving money too. Check your handbook – my washing machine at 20°C uses a third of the energy of a 40°C wash of the same duration and same water – 90 per cent of the energy is used to heat the water.

For the best results, after laundering dry the items outside in the fresh air. I always give wet items a good shake before hanging them out – this helps to remove creases, lifts pile on fluffy items such as towels and helps them to dry soft. Even if the weather is dull and cold and there is not much wind, as my grandmother would say: 'As long as the paths, drive and pavements are dry, your laundry will certainly lighten and can even dry.' Fact.

To avoid fusty smells developing on even the cleanest of laundry, I never put clean clothes, towels or bedding away in cupboards, drawers and wardrobes straight away. The clean items should be aired first to ensure that everything is completely dry. A slightly damp seam or hem, or residual moisture left by a steam iron are all recipes for a fusty result if put away without airing.

Back in the day I always used to use a clothes horse to dry clothes, as did my grandmother before me, and I used to believe as a child it was a household item used only for drying the washing around the coal fire on a wet day. The clothes horse (a slatted, wooden, folding gate-type construction, often joined together with a thick wadding-type fabric) could be opened up to become a huge freestanding piece of kit. I remember as a child it could double up as a great tent out in the garden with a sheet laid over, but I also remember the huge disappointment when arriving home from school on the coldest of Mondays (always wash day), to find the clothes horse adorned with wet washing and wrapped around the fireplace. The coal fire was roaring yet the room felt cold, as the clothes horse had grabbed the best place and warmest spot in the room.

As well as an aid to dry the laundry indoors, the clothes horse was also used to air the laundry to prevent any mould, mildew and odours. Laundry would be dried outside, ironed until completely smooth, then folded into a neat arrangement with the larger items on the lower runners and smaller items further up. My grandmother would have the colours together and the whites boasting their brightness together, all dazzling in crisp, clean perfectness.

Clothes would be left to air for a day indoors before being put away. A vintage wooden clothes horse I now consider a thing of beauty; I don't have one but I do have a wooden ceiling rack that both dries the laundry on wet days and displays my ironing, which is also left to air overnight.

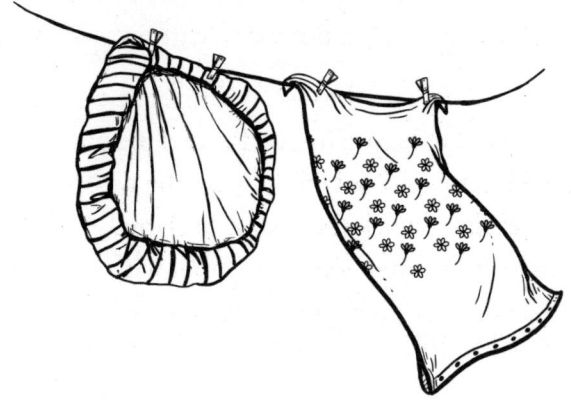

Avoid faded lines on clothing

Ever washed a new pair of jeans or trousers to find that once dry there are what can be best described as faded lines left on the fabric after drying? The main message here is to avoid the hot wash, biological detergents and the powerful spin of the washing machine. A new pair of black or denim jeans can quickly lose their rich dark colour even after their first wash. Excess spin speeds will force the items into deep creases that are then pushed to the sides of the machine drum while it does its job of extracting as much water as possible from the clothing. The trouble is, the clothing items are new and this fast, brutal action will not only extract as much water as possible, it will also force fabric dye out.

I have a couple of routines that I apply to my treasured items of clothing, particularly dark colours, such as navy, black and reds.

You will need

large sink or bowl big enough to soak the item(s)

1 part vinegar
2 parts cold water (for example 500ml (17fl oz) of white vinegar and 1 litre (1¾ pints) of cold water)

In a large sink, add the vinegar and cold water. Before the first ever wash of the garment, turn the item inside out, lay it into the solution and leave for a few hours or overnight. This will help to fix the dye. As already mentioned, I always wash on a cold 20°C, which reduces any fabric colour runs.

When it comes to the first wash, err on the side of caution. Use my woollens detergent and washing instructions (see page 206), and preferably wash by hand and drip-dry outside – then there is little or no risk of colour fading, getting lines from the spinner, or shrinkage.

For general washing thereafter, ask yourself these questions:

1. Does this item actually need washing? Can I instead turn the item inside out and simply hang it outside to freshen up? This will remove cooking smells, tobacco, etc. If the weather isn't fine, try a spray of my Easy Breeze fabric spray (see page 235) to refresh without washing.

2. If the item is very precious, avoid the machine altogether and use a cool hand wash and drip dry.

3. If a machine wash is necessary, turn the garment inside out and wash on a cold 20°C. And to avoid those telltale spin lines, reduce the spin speed or time.

Bronzer and sun cream stains on clothing

Sun creams, bronzing and tanning products have become daily essentials for many to enhance or protect their skin's appearance at different times of the year. Sun creams offer protection against the sun's harmful rays in the summer months, while bronzing and tanning products promise to give the skin a 'sun-kissed' glow at other times when the sun has stopped shining. Thank goodness products and information are much more advanced than they were.

Not until the 1960s did the first instance of SPF (sun protection factor) appear. However, the amount added to suntan lotions was incredibly low, the products were quite expensive and people would make their own skin frizzlers rather than skin protectors.

I can remember my first foreign holiday by bus to Spain in the 1970s. An exciting time – no sun cream was needed, just a handy bottle of a home-made mix of olive oil and vinegar smothered all over and I was beach ready for day one of my holiday in the powerful Mediterranean sun.

Days two and three I was so badly burnt I had to stay indoors.

The look in the 1970s and 1980s was to go home from your first foreign holiday looking like a chargrilled red pepper. This was a true indication to everyone back at home that you had had a great holiday! Knowing and understanding much more about sun damage to skin, premature ageing, drying, burning and, at worse, higher risk of cancers results in more and more of us reaching for sun protection.

However, like everything, the more we know, the more there is to know, and I would not have favoured any particular brand when shopping. I would choose a high factor and I particularly liked to see that the ingredients on my latest purchase were vegan, sustainable and dermatologically tested.

It was not until I went on holiday very recently and read the hotel information booklet, which featured a paragraph on sun protection products. Here's a quote from it: 'While on site here please avoid using any lotion containing the hormone-disrupting chemical Avobenzone – it is harmful to yourself, to the coral reef and to your clothing.' I was surprised and shocked – I had no idea about the harmful effect of the chemicals in my sun protection and had a look at the long list (Octinoxate, Octocrylene and Cyclopentasiloxane – to name just a few). So I started to do some reading around and found that there are many other chemicals and studies have already shown a particularly high level of toxicity in early life-stage fish. Some are also suspected of contributing to coral bleaching, and it has been detected throughout the marine food chain. Some products have been banned in other countries. This really is a minefield and I spent hours when I should have been writing this book trying to get my head around what one should do. My advice: do your research – there are independent apps available that will help you to make an informed choice – no paid ads and brand promotions.

I felt let down that my product scored 'Bad' at 1/100 because of the use of the chemicals stated above, when it promised me 'sustainable ingredients' and supported cancer charities – all marketing magic. To make matters even worse, it caused terrific staining on clothing, and there was no warning about this on the bottle.

From the list of questions I receive daily – and especially during the summer months – sun cream stains rank in the top 5. These can be troublesome because the ingredients can differ, so the stain treatments need to be varied, if at first you don't succeed.

My biggest challenge to date came after returning from holiday. The non-greasy, clear, easy-to-apply and water-resistant SPF30 Once a Day sun protection gel I had invested in sounded perfect on the packet. Once home and the holiday laundry was sorted into piles, the washing machine started its marathon stint. Little did I know the whites were in for a marathon stint too.

I will list here the various stages I went through before stain removal was complete, though your sun cream may not be so stubborn and a pre-soak may be all that is necessary. For others with the most difficult stains, you should get there in the end. A pile of soiled, well-travelled holiday whites, including white shirts, a sports top, a white dress and underwear with grubby collars, a few food spills, general dirt and staining from daily wear, yet there were no sun cream stains to be seen – yet. The sun protection being used was, of course, a clear gel. Below is a step-by-step, sun cream stain treatment guide that should dissolve even the worst cases of staining.

Stage one: overnight soak

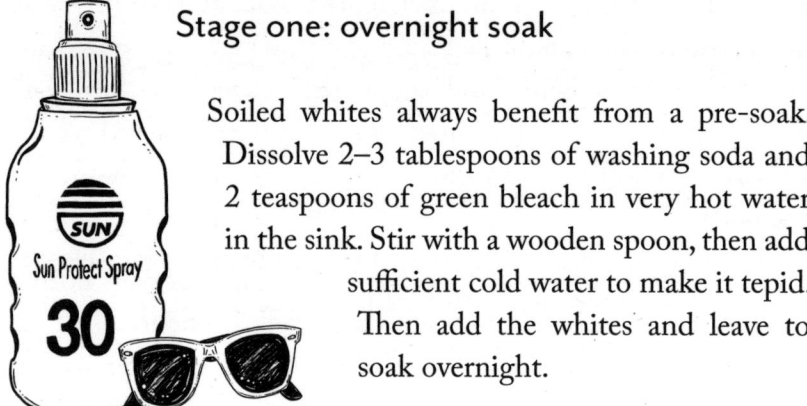

Soiled whites always benefit from a pre-soak. Dissolve 2–3 tablespoons of washing soda and 2 teaspoons of green bleach in very hot water in the sink. Stir with a wooden spoon, then add sufficient cold water to make it tepid. Then add the whites and leave to soak overnight.

Stage two: wash

Choose a long, 20°C eco-wash cycle using 100ml (3½fl oz) of my own detergent into a plastic cup straight into the drum (see page 202), plus 2 tablespoons of washing soda in the detergent drawer, to soften the water and 2 tablespoons of my own fabric softener (see page 200) in the dispenser.

Back to the laundry, I could not believe it! The general grime present before washing had dissolved but been replaced in different parts of the clothing by yellow stains caused by the sun cream. The stains were on the insides of clothing, around the collars, the insides of the button-up fastenings, under the arms and some noticeable heavy streaking where a tight-fitting sports shirt had suffered when being pulled over a hot sweaty body. As the sun was shining, I pegged the washing out anyway, hoping the stains would fade, but they didn't.

Stage three: cream cleaner

Back indoors with my dried and still-stained laundry, I decided to apply my 'washed-in' grease stain treatment. This is a great routine for when a stain hasn't come out in the wash. It can dissolve washed-in, very old grease stains.

Wet the stained area with water, massage in my cream cleaner (see page 11), then place the items in a plastic bag so that they don't dry out, and leave overnight.

Next day I washed the items again – a full load of sun protection victims – to find that although the stains had faded a little, the problem was still very evident and the clothes couldn't be worn again in their present state.

Stage four: Pure Magic

I added 2–3 tablespoons of Pure Magic (see page 7) to a bucket, filled to three-quarters full with cold water, then soaked the items for 15 minutes.

The sun was shining again, thankfully, so I trusted Mother Nature to finish the job for me. Outside, without rinsing, I pegged the laundry out in full sun and left the items to drip dry.

Magically, when all else failed – Pure Magic and free sunshine returned my very stained items to their former glory. I didn't wash or rinse again, though you may wish to rinse the items again to remove any residual Pure Magic that may have left clothing feeling a bit stiff to the touch.

If the stains are on dark or coloured clothing you can follow the same treatment. One of my items was a polo shirt – navy blue at the back and collar and white at the front and sleeves. The treatment was exactly the same, for the greasy-looking stain on the navy blue and yellow stains on the white. After the soak and drip dry the Pure Magic had left a few white crusty blobs on the navy collar. I rinsed the dried and stain-free top in cold water and the Pure Magic residue disappeared.

For the future

I really would like to save me (and you) from this gruelling stain-removal marathon, but the problem is that not all sun creams, bronzers and fake tans are made with the same ingredients, and while many stains will respond to my cream cleaner pre-treatment before the first ever wash, others, as in my case, didn't even show themselves until after washing. The clear gel left no marks on clothing at the outset – but my promise of Once a Day Sun Protection resulted in two days of stain removal.

Baby poosplosion

I am sure all parents will be familiar with the situation – those baby bottom explosions and not knowing really where to start. My babies had reusable terry towelling nappies with a reusable soft linen liner that went next to the skin. Disposable nappies I don't think were even a thing.

Nothing gave me more pleasure than a line of clean nappies blowing in the wind – white nappies, baby clothes and even white curtain nets were considered a thing of beauty and, unfortunately, something a young mother and housewife would be judged on. Woe betides those whose whites were considered under par – the nosy neighbours would make sure you got a mention over the garden fence! 'If her nets are that grey, what must the bed sheets be like?'

Then came the disposable nappy, which took over the market. This was great. When I looked after my grandchildren when they were babies, I was delighted at how convenient the nappy situation was. Yet again, as time travels on and with more information to hand, it is evident that the environmental impact of single-use nappies is much higher than for a reusable nappy.

I would not preach to anyone about what to do – my babies had reusable, my grandchildren had single-use before we knew so much about the issue of production costs, fatbergs in sewers from flushing liners (and even nappies) and the dumping of all of these products into landfill.

I know, however, from the number of questions I receive, that more and more people are turning to reusable nappies and having a pack of single-use for trips out and holidays. Maybe that is a great compromise.

I have memories of picking up my first baby and not really knowing where to start – baby poo everywhere! First exit was usually up the back and down the legs, then other seepages through clothing, onto towels, the changing mat, and usually the baby would be gurgling and happy having recovered from a likely tummy ache.

But how to get those reusable nappies really clean? The parents reading this know all too well that the stains are not confined to the nappy – there's the sleep suit or day clothes, the bedding, towels, plus very often your own clothes – a poosplosion has no limits.

NATURE'S FREEBIE: Full sunshine can bleach out many baby poo stains even after washing. Hang the clean but still-stained items outside in full sun and Mother Nature will finish the job for you.

When the sun doesn't shine, it is often necessary to dissolve the stains before washing. Some parents and carers will have their own system for very stained items, but for those looking for advice, this method below should help.

Save up a load of nappies, though, to be honest, with a new baby in the house the washing machine will go on often. When I used terry nappies and liners I used to rinse the soiled items in cold water, then add them to a bucket of clean cold water with washing soda and save them up until I had a full load. Washing 'present-day' reusable nappies, I would do exactly the same.

A washing soda solution is a natural de-greaser, odour neutralizer, water softener and anti-bac cleaner, which will not only help to dissolve the stains before washing, but the nappy bucket will not get smelly. This method can also be used during the very messy weaning stages when those soft-staining foods are hard to remove from clothes – avocado, orange and melon come to mind.

You will need

FOR THE PRE-SOAK BUCKET

bucket

wooden spoon

2–3 tbsp washing soda

Add the washing soda and a little hot water to the bucket, then stir to dissolve. Fill up with cold water until the water is tepid. Add the rinsed nappies or stained clothes and keep adding until there are enough for a load.

Once there are sufficient to make up a load, squeeze the excess water out of the items and put them straight into the washing machine.

TO WASH

2–3 tbsp washing soda
2 tsp green bleach
100ml (3½fl oz) detergent (see page 202)
2–3 tbsp fabric softener (see page 200)

I choose a long eco cycle at 20°C, as hot water can actually fix some stains. Pre-soaking and using washing soda and green bleach in the wash, plus air drying, work perfectly for me.

If you prefer to use a hot wash, that's entirely up to you, though my experience is that stains are more likely to dissolve during cold washing, colours stay brighter and fewer plastics are released into the waterways. The exception for me is where there have been any illnesses like vomiting and diarrhoea, when a hotter wash may be advisable.

Try to avoid overloading the washing machine drum – the items need room to move around, be picked up and dropped into the water and be agitated in a way that would be done by hand or in the old-fashioned twin-tub machines. My washing machine drum is 45cm (18in) in diameter and, as a rough guide, once the laundry is loaded into the drum I put one hand inside on top of my dry laundry and if I have around one-third of the space left above it (15cm/6in) then I consider I have sufficient room for my laundry to move freely and efficiently.

Air-dry where possible – when the weather doesn't permit, I use a ceiling-hung drying rack. I gather most reusable nappies shouldn't go into the tumble dryer as it can harm their absorbency.

Bubble stains and stubborn baby stains that have escaped the routine above are probably worth a mention here as I receive so many queries. The scenario is: items have been washed and soaked as above yet still stubborn stains remain. They have been left out in the sunshine but no luck – the dreaded bubble mix and some baby stains can be very stubborn.

My advice here is to place the items into a large bowl or bucket, add 2–3 teaspoons of green bleach and 2–3 tablespoons of washing soda and pour over the hottest water until the items are submerged. The solution will foam, so use the handle of a wooden spoon to keep everything under the water line, then leave to soak overnight. The next day, a rinse either by hand or machine should reveal clean, stain-free garments. I refuse to give up and I usually get there in the end – the exception always being permanent ink. I guess it does what it says on the tin!

Slime stains

Slime is a relatively new product and thankfully one that hadn't been developed when my own kids were small. The chemical substance, simply put, is a tactile and sensory play tool that is used by children and adults alike. It is supposed to help to relieve stress, unwind and relax. However, any benefits could be reversed if the user manages to stain clothing and upholstery! I have had so many cries for help from parents faced with slime dropped onto carpets, onto furniture and all over clothing. This sticky substance is often brightly coloured and scented too.

For clothing

An overnight soak usually does the trick.

You will need

large bowl or sink
wooden spoon

2–3 tbsp washing soda
2 tsp green bleach (optional)

500ml (17fl oz) hot water
1.5 litres (2½ pints) cold water

Add the washing soda to a bowl or sink with the green bleach, if using (see Note). Then add the hot water, stirring with a wooden spoon until the powder has dissolved and the solution is cloudy. The wooden spoon will receive a quick anti-bac clean too.

Once dissolved, add the cold water – the soaking solution should feel neither hot nor cold. Add then the slime-stained garment. Leave to soak in the tepid solution overnight.

Next day, put the item in a long 20°C eco, cold wash cycle and the stains will dissolve.

NOTE: If the slime is brightly coloured and there is a risk that the colour may stain too, add green bleach to the soak at the same time as the washing soda, dissolving it in the hot water.

For carpets and upholstery

You will need

small bowl
clean cotton pad or small cloth

Basic Magic solution – about 100ml (3½fl oz)
  (see page 43)

Put my Basic Magic solution into a small bowl and soak a cotton pad or cloth in it. Dab at the stain with the solution and work from the outside inwards to prevent spreading the stain further. Do not rub or scrub, as this can damage fibres and carpet/furniture pile.

Always test a small area first (for colour fastness and to see how it dries) and do not over-wet the stain.

Brighten the bling!

Low-cost fun jewellery is great, but it can soon tarnish and look dull. I have a necklace with brightly coloured enamelled shapes that are secured by a chain. I used to wear it a lot but then it went out of favour. I decided to wear it with a white dress to go out – I thought the colours could show themselves off – so on it went and I thought it looked fine. As the evening wore on I could smell a metal odour, but didn't think much about it until I got home to see the chain had left a black mark around my neck! The smell I had detected was obviously tarnish from the chain. Here's how I got rid of that for future uses.

You will need

shallow bowl
old toothbrush
clean water
soft cloth

Pure Magic (see page 7)

Lay the item in a shallow bowl, spray over Pure Magic to cover all parts and leave to soak for about half an hour. Use the old toothbrush to then get into tiny nooks and crannies before rinsing it in clean warm water. Leave to dry on a soft cloth.

Pure Magic is great for fashion jewellery – it will quickly brighten it up, remove any tarnish and make it sing again.

Sandals and sliders

When the sun shines, last summer's sandals and sliders reappear and, sadly, they may look a bit 'last year' too. My cream cleaner will do an excellent job of whipping them back into shape, whether they be leather, suede or plastic.

You will need

cloth
toothbrush

cream cleaner (see page 11)
Pure Magic (see page 7, optional, for stained white footwear)

Use a damp cloth to wipe over the sandal, then massage in my cream cleaner, paying special attention to the grubby parts. An old toothbrush can be useful for difficult-to-reach areas. Do not overwet the shoe; allow the cream cleaner to do its work for about an hour, then wipe off using a warm damp cloth. Leave outside in full sunshine to whiten and brighten if they are pale in colour, otherwise air-dry in the shade.

Once completely dried, brush off any excess dry powder.

White footwear can be brightened even further using just a tiny spritz of Pure Magic – sprayed on, wiped with a damp cloth to ensure an even covering, then left in full sun.

I recall a cry for help from a follower who had smashed a whole jar of pasta sauce onto the floor in the supermarket. She was wearing white trainers! After cleaning off as much as possible – Pure Magic, a little water and an old toothbrush used to brush it in and foam it up, wipe clear with a damp cloth and then leave out in full sunshine for Mother Nature to finish the job!

PERSONAL AND PETS

There are so many personal cleaning products – too many to mention – creams, lotions, shampoos and perfumes, and the same goes for our pets too. There is a product for anything we can think of – it is a huge industry and one I am stepping into very slowly, tending to err on the side of caution because I realize that what suits one person may not suit another. However, I have a little bag of recipes here that I use routinely – they work well, obviously mixed at home, and I would like to share them with you.

Liquid hand soap

My infant recipe – so-called because I have learned so much since its debut. When I first developed the recipe it was made using used soap slivers – ends of soaps that may otherwise have been thrown away. Feedback from users over time, however, presented me with a few issues. The liquid soap, while starting off well, could thicken and/or separate in the bottle, and then it was difficult to get it to pump through the dispenser. Even though it was easily fixed by topping up the soap with a little more just-boiled water and giving it a good shake, it set my mind to work on how to improve this recipe given the number of plastic soap dispenser bottles that a household would get through in one year. I have since found out that soaps differ tremendously, so I decided it was better to stick with a list of specific ingredients.

There are many 500ml (17fl oz) bottles of liquid hand soap available on the market, and the list of chemicals on the reverse label can be astounding. They are often brightly coloured and highly perfumed; some can be expensive while others are worryingly cheap!

I wanted to use natural unperfumed soap because it was apparent that using a variety of soap brands, perfumes and ingredients was giving me inconsistent results. Natural soap flakes are available online and in certain supermarkets (especially in France) and by adding a few additional ingredients that 'green cleaners' already have to hand I was able to put together a stable creamy soap that would behave itself in a pump dispenser. I have found some porcelain pump dispensers available, if you prefer that to reusing plastic ones.

Here's how to make 500ml (17fl oz) liquid hand soap from just 25g (¾oz) natural soap flakes.

You will need

1 litre (34fl oz) heatproof jug
small whisk or spoon
hand-held blender
funnel (optional)
scales
500ml (17fl oz) used soap bottle with pump dispenser

- 50g (1¾oz) bicarbonate of soda (natural cleaner)
- 50ml (1¾fl oz) vegetable glycerine (cleans and is kind to the skin)
- 15ml (1 tbsp) unperfumed eco-friendly washing-up liquid (emulsifier)
- 25g (¾oz) natural (e.g. Marseille) unperfumed soap flakes or a bar of soap that can be grated or finely sliced into slivers. Slicing soap is very satisfying – a bit like crumbling cheese.
- ¼ tsp xanthan gum (thickener)
- 250–300ml (8–10fl oz) warm, recently boiled water (diluent)
- 10–20 drops of non-acidic essential oil (optional – I like clean linen, ylang ylang, honeysuckle, sandalwood, calendula and rose, though I am still experimenting with new scents)
- 2–3 drops of soap or food colouring (optional)

Place the empty jug onto the scales, weigh out the bicarbonate of soda, vegetable glycerine, washing-up liquid, soap flakes or slithers and xanthan gum, resetting to zero between each ingredient and transferring each to the jug. Mix to a thick smooth paste using a small whisk or spoon.

Gradually add the hot water 100ml (3½fl oz) at a time, stirring between each addition. The soap will thicken.

Once 250ml (9fl oz) has been added, blitz until thick and smooth using the blender, then leave to stand and cool. I needed the extra

50ml (1¾fl oz) to thin down to a thick pouring consistency, but see how yours is once cold.

It needs to be the consistency of thick pouring cream. Once you have the desired consistency, add perfume and soap colouring to tint, if using. I use sandalwood, given it is non-acidic and in no danger of clumping the soap, and a few drops of lemon soap colour gives a pale primrose tint. Use a funnel if it's easier, or pour straight into the bottle, then screw in the pump attachment. I keep mine alongside the kitchen sink for hand washing. If it does happen to thicken further in the dispenser I simply top up with water, give it a shake and continue.

Save your soap

Soap slivers, those ends of soaps that in my youth used to be fused together to make a bigger bar, are probably nowadays tossed into the bin once they become wafer thin, devoid of any perfume and too small to create a lather. However, if you have enjoyed a bar of natural (maybe expensive) soap, or like me you get a thrill from making something out of nothing, this one may well suit you. I save ends of soaps (slivers) in a pretty jar in the bathroom and maybe once a year or so have a soap-making session with the grandchildren. I mentioned this in a previous book, but since then I have gone on to improve the recipe, method and outcome, achieving, I think, a better-quality soap.

This is a simple gift idea for children to make. My grandchildren enjoy making small heart-shaped soaps, Christmas-themed soaps – the possibilities are endless. Wrapped in coloured tissue papers or popped into a paper box or small organza bags, you have the perfect simple little gift from ends of soaps that would have been destined for the bin. Win-win!

You will need

- small saucepan
- small grater or small food processor (my hand blender has a mini processor as an attachment) or wooden board and knife
- small heatproof bowl
- wooden spoon
- silicone moulds

- 50g (1¾oz) soap slivers (or use any weight of end of soaps, adding 10 per cent of their weight in boiling water)
- 1 tbsp just-boiled water
- 1–2 drops of soap or food colouring of choice
- 3–5 drops of essential oil

Place a small saucepan of water on the heat, bring to the boil, then reduce to a simmer.

Grate the soap as finely as possible or chop on a chopping board – the best results are achieved if the soap is roughly chopped or grated then blitzed to a fine powder in the food processor.

Transfer the powdered soap to the bowl, add the small quantity of just-boiled water, then the soap or food colouring followed by essential oil for perfume.

Place the bowl over the pan of simmering water and just leave it ticking over very slowly. I have seen people use the microwave to melt the soap, but I prefer this 'bain-marie' method for a smooth soap. The soap powder will slowly melt and can then be stirred to ensure that the colour and perfume is well mixed. Once smooth and a runny consistency, pour into the moulds and leave to set for a couple of hours in a cool place. Once solid, turn out of the moulds and the soap is ready to use.

Home-made deodorant

When I think of the smells around me when growing up – my grandmother's house was sparkling clean and the familiar smells would be fresh bread in the kitchen, Cussons Imperial Leather soap in the bathroom and she always had a bottle of odourless witch hazel, which she said I had to dab on my teenage spots. She also gave me a little talk about body odour and suggested I wipe under the arms with witch hazel, as that would prevent any smells. It was also my grandad's aftershave and that was the 'go to' for soothing insect bites. In other words, that one bottle was a good all-rounder.

I did some research around deodorants because their introduction and development interested me so much, maybe because I can recall the time when they were not even around.

Apparently, not until the 1950s was deodorant available as a 'roll on', and then in the late 1960s the first aerosol antiperspirant was introduced. They were only put on the market for women – men's deodorants were not even a thing.

I remember spray deodorants becoming widely available in the 1970s and I couldn't get enough of it! I used lots and lots, then came the handbag size, so I was spraying and breathing it in constantly! Never ever did I think a time would come when I would want to go back to witch hazel. I hated it at the time – much preferring the new modern pungent perfumes and sprays.

However, fast-forward 50 years and the message now is very different. We understand that aerosol deodorants contain propellants like propane and butane that are harmful to the environment. The concern for me is the effect of on the scented chemicals directly on the skin and in the air around me. I was actually forcing the chemicals into my body via the skin, then at the same time inevitably breathing it all in too. I have dispensed with proprietary perfumes and deodorants and am happy with my little home-made deodorant spray.

Roll-on deodorants are available, but rather than go into too much detail about the chemicals that I have read are used to keep body odour at bay, that then wash off into the water system and pollute rivers, I will keep it simple by saying I have switched back to witch hazel. Witch hazel is a plant with proven medicinal benefits – a bottle of natural distillate made from the plant is a natural astringent with anti-inflammatory properties and is inexpensive.

Spray deodorant

As an experiment, and to put witch hazel through its paces, one very hot day when I was to be working in the garden I sprayed under one arm using only witch hazel with no perfume. At the end of the day I had one neutral armpit and one not so pleasant, and I was delighted at the outcome.

I wanted to test my deodorant spray further, so I gifted a bottle to my much younger friend who said she doubted it would work for her, because she knows she has a perspiration problem, along with my 16-year-old 'gym-obsessed' granddaughter. Be honest, I said, and let me know how it goes. They were straight back to me – they loved it. One was given the spray and the other the roll-on. Needless to say, I now keep myself and all of my granddaughters supplied with deodorants. I use distilled witch hazel (often unperfumed) as an underarm spray daily.

You will need

> used small glass spray bottle – mine is 25ml (¾fl oz)
> small funnel
>
> distilled witch hazel
> 2 drops of essential oil (optional) – try clean linen,

honeysuckle, ylang ylang, rose, or for men, sandalwood, bergamot, orange, coconut

Magic Mixer (1–2 drops polysorbate 80 or slightest drizzle of honey or glucose)

Fill the bottle with the witch hazel, add the essential oil for perfume, if desired, and the Magic Mixer to fully blend. Shake well and it is ready to use.

Note – if using witch hazel on its own there is no need for the Magic Mixer, which is used only as an emulsifier.

NOTE: Witch hazel is generally considered a safe and natural product, but for those with very sensitive skin, try a patch test before using.

Roll-on deodorant

Roll-on deodorants I believe are a little less harmful in terms of the environment because of their packaging and negating the need for an aerosol spray. The deodorant can be applied exactly where needed, so there is no waste, yet the worrying factor for me was the ingredients list.

In one case I read that the roll-on I was using sounded great because it contained aloe vera, but it also contained, amongst others, a chemical BHT (butylated hydroxytoluene), which is a compound used in cosmetics for its antioxidant function (in essence, I think, to stop it going off). I read on to then discover it can affect thyroid function, fertility and development, and can be found in the placenta and breast milk. This chemical is also very toxic to marine life.

This is another example of how clever marketing has us believing that the product contains a natural ingredient, only to read on to understand that the percentage of good ingredients can very often be outnumbered by a large percentage of harmful hidden ingredients. I had to come up with a simple home-made recipe that would be effective, lightly scented and, most of all, safe.

I used empty (often plastic) roll-on bottles for this, though once I made the permanent switch to greener living I invested in 50ml (1¾fl oz) reusable, glass roll-on bottles and used the higher measure of ingredients below. Container sizes differ, so I have given 2 or 3 tablespoon measures, depending on pack size, though I have found it is better to have some head room so that the mix can be shaken well to combine.

You will need

1 empty (often plastic) roll-on bottle
measuring spoons

3–4 tbsp witch hazel
½–1 tbsp vegetable glycerine
¼–½ tsp sea salt
3–5 drops of essential oil of choice – optional

(honeysuckle, ylang ylang, lemon, or try 3 drops of calendula and 2 drops of rose for something I consider very pleasing)

Removing the roll-on ball from a used container is straightforward, as the plastic ball easily comes away from its housing. Hold on to the roller ball and gently twist to one side, then, once removed, it can be washed, the container de-labelled and dried thoroughly.

Measure the ingredients into the container, fix the roller ball and give it a good shake. The salt crystals will dissolve within the hour.

As the solution is thinner than commercial roll-on deodorants, or if the roller ball is large, to apply I give the container a shake then hold it upright (not upside-down) and apply it to the under arm. There is sufficient liquid on the roller ball for the application. Holding the container upside down to roll can discharge a little too much.

I have to say my brown glass bottles have a small roller ball that is just right and can be used any way – upright or tilted.

About the ingredients and why I included them:

Witch hazel is a natural astringent, which means it removes excess moisture from the skin, it neutralizes odour, is anti-inflammatory, kills bacteria and on further research, I realize, is used in many natural skincare products.

Vegetable glycerine helps to thicken the solution and emulsify the perfume oil. It is also a fixative, meaning that it will hold the fragrance together for longer by slowing down its evaporation. Glycerine is kind to the skin and is used in many skincare products.

I have included sea salt in the recipe because I read it is widely used in many proprietary natural deodorant products. It helps to neutralize and destroy odour-causing bacteria and is a well-known preservative.

Essential oils add a hint of perfume; I choose sustainable natural essential oils.

As for the shelf life of these products: I alternate daily between spray and roll-on and they both are fine until used up – around 4–6 months. If you decide to keep things very simple and use just witch hazel, the shelf life is the same as the product – 12 months. Another advantage about making your own spray and roll-on is that they do not stain clothes.

Body spray

I fell totally in love with the simplicity and ease of my deodorants, so much so that I mixed in larger quantities, changed up the perfume and made a light and lovely body spray. No more aerosol sprays, throw-away cans and cannisters, and there is something about the clean fragrance that I enjoy. There is also no residual stale perfume odour on clothing – I am loving it. Maybe it's a handy little gift idea, too.

You will need

small funnel
100ml (3½fl oz) glass spray bottle (or reuse a bottle of choice)

- 90ml (3fl oz) distilled witch hazel
- 8 drops of essential oil (my current favourite is calendula and rose)
- Magic Mixer (8 drops polysorbate 80 or small drizzle of honey or glucose) (see page 14)

Add the witch hazel to the bottle followed by the other ingredients. Shake to emulsify, then it is ready to use. Shelf life is a few months, by which time it is used up. I prefer to mix this up in small quantities so that the perfume remains fresh.

Strengthen your tights

Can you believe I can remember when tights replaced stockings? At secondary school, in the final year, we were allowed to wear nylon stockings and we were given a lesson on how to safely put on fine stockings by rolling them up the leg without catching or laddering, and to then fasten them to the suspender belt. Hilarious! Then, suddenly, still in that final year of 1970, girls started to wear tights – I am sure we called them pantyhose to begin with. These were fantastic and the headmistress, I fear, was now losing her grip on this generation of girls that didn't want the ladders, saggy wrinkled nylons and the rubber-buttoned suspenders. I remember my first pair – they were new and expensive, of course (a bit like colour televisions at that time). I treasured my newly acquired trendy piece of kit that had cost me 9s 11d (about 50p). All the schoolgirls were sporting their tights and mini-skirts, but the only trouble was, rather than ladder, they sprang holes. Soon the girls, not having the funds to replace their tights, would sew up the holes using natural-coloured thread. Then came a great tip – freeze your tights before their first wear.

You will need

brand new stockings or tights
small plastic bag
freezer

Not having done this for 50 years, and not really knowing whether it truly was effective back in the day, I put it to the test. I had a brand-new pair of fine hold-ups – never been worn. I wet one sock with cold water, squeezed it out, then put it into a bag and into the freezer. To be honest, I forgot about it until 2 days later, but then I retrieved it from the shelf when I was really searching for a tub of frozen home-made soup. I removed the stocking from its bag and left it to thaw. Once thawed it soon dried naturally, then I was able to put it to the test.

I decided a tough test would be to ease the stockings over a coarse box grater, starting with the stocking that hadn't been frozen. Oh dear, the stocking was laddered, caught on the metal holes and really was a mess. Then for the previously frozen stocking, which eased over the metal grater just the same. To my surprise the nylon was more robust – a catch here and a catch there when I tried to remove it, but no ladders or holes. It really did work! So having my new tights slotted amongst the ice cubes in the tiny freezer compartment of the fridge back in 1970 really did make a difference!

Is this something I would routinely do nowadays? Probably not, though if I had invested in a pair of very fine and expensive 10-denier tights to be worn for a special occasion I would definitely make the effort, to save any annoying and embarrassing snags or ladders that could be seen when I take to the dance floor at a wedding.

> **TIP:** Rather than discard your laddered tights and stockings – freeze them. Once frozen they are much easier to cut into neat slices with scissors. Once completely thawed the neat bands of nylon can be used as plant ties, hair ties or really can be put to any use where an elastic band would be called for.

Pet-friendly cleaning

Those of us with pets will be comfortable knowing the products we use around them are not harmful. As we continue to use natural products around the home, there are still a couple of troublesome areas that I'm often asked about.

Pet bedding

Many have asked about how to wash pet bedding without leaving traces of pet hair in the washing machine that may damage it, but also when the next washing load goes in, the hairs then stick to clothing. I have an old single bed quilt cover – I pop the dog bed inside, zip it up, then wash it as normal. I choose a windy dry day when I can then take the lot outside.

Unzip or unbutton the quilt cover, remove the dog bed and peg out onto the line. The quilt cover is then turned inside out, where any loose hair will have been contained. That is pinned onto the washing line, too, and as the cover dries, the pet hair will blow off.

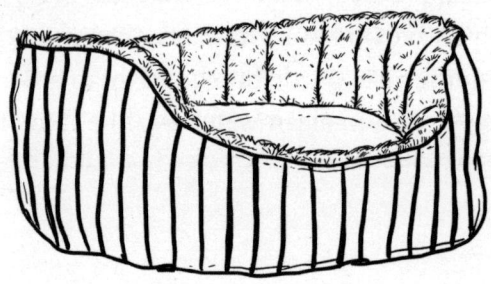

Cleaning imitation grass

I have had a number of queries about how imitation grass should be cleaned to remove pet urine odour, and concrete areas, too, for those without a green space for their pets to use as a toilet.

I don't have this problem, though I have offered advice to many and this works well.

Bicarbonate of soda can be sprinkled over an area, brushed in and then simply left for Mother Nature to rinse off if rain is forecast. Bicarbonate of soda is not toxic and will effectively neutralize any odours and clean it up a treat too.

Drinking bowls, feeders and food bowls

A hot washing soda soak will dissolve any residual foods and stains from feeding bowls. Dissolve 2–3 tablespoons of washing soda in a bowl or bucket of hot water, submerge the bowls in it and leave overnight, then add to a simple wash the next day.

Water bowls and feeders of all types for birds and small pets can become green and water-scaled. Spray these with Pure Magic (see page 7) and leave on for 15 minutes, then finish with a scrub using an old toothbrush, bottle brush or loofah scourer for hard-to-reach areas. A rinse in clean water and the items are like new again.

Litter trays

I don't have cats, but my followers use 2–3 tablespoons of Basic Magic (see page 43) in warm water to wash between refills. Its natural anti-bacterial and odour-busting qualities do a perfect job.

CONCLUSION

As I am ready to close this – my seventh book (can you believe?) – I say to myself, is this it? Has the green journey, transformation, lifestyle change, or whatever you want to call it come to a natural end? My answer to that is – absolutely not! As with anything in life, the more you know, the more there is to know.

I am entering my second 'green' decade and when I look back at how much more I now understand than I did at the start I realize how much is lodged into my head and just has to be set down into words. I have gained so much knowledge and experience during this time. I find that as my message continues to gather pace, readers and followers are deciding that they too are wanting to question, query and change – which is great!

My time, and in fact my life's work nowadays is spent forever critically examining, searching and discovering problems and threats to our health and the health of our planet. Some worrying issues may be going unnoticed but that then is a trigger for me to set out researching and looking at ways of presenting natural solutions where possible.

Going green for me has been a thorough lifestyle change. I have turned my back on modern methods of cleaning which as we know so often involve toxic chemicals, fumes and hazards, not to mention the plastic bottles and single-use packaging. I have said so many times that going green is addictive in a feel-good way. It is liberating, definitely cheaper and as well as being better for my health, the health of my family and our precious earth – and fundamentally, it works!

From the number of before-and-after success stories, great feedback and reviews, it is clear that so many of us are delighted with our green lifestyle and homemade alternatives and although I have written a collection of books on the subject and I continue to strive to do my very best, let's not forget it is you the readers that will make the difference.

Each and every one of you, in your own kitchens, can do this although it may at first seem daunting – it is after all a lifestyle change. However, as with any change of habit, before you know where you are you will be doing things differently without spending more time as each and every recipe and process becomes familiar. My recipes and tips are tried and tested and how fantastic to no longer add cleaning products onto the weekly shopping list because there is a simple multipurpose store in the cupboard at home.

Let us make chemical-heavy, toxic cleaning a thing of the past. Better for our own health, the health of our children, saves us money and as a result ultimately our precious planet can breathe a sigh of relief.

Thank you for reading *Clean Magic* and I hope that as well as introducing new ingredients, methods, recipes and ideas I have also been able to polish to perfection some of my original everyday products. I hope like me you now feel even better equipped to embrace an even greener lifestyle without any confusion.

Feeling inspired? Let's do this!

ACKNOWLEDGEMENTS

My writing time is early morning – sometimes as early at 5a.m. – and other than Wilfred and Rose my faithful dogs laid sleeping at my feet, it can seem a fairly solitary affair.

However, once a basic manuscript has taken shape, I know I can rely on the people around me to support, direct, timetable, check, proofread, illustrate, design, edit, publicise and take over all of the other necessary tasks that go into writing a book.

The people I would like to thank are many.

My friends and agents at Yellow Poppy Media who have supported me for over a decade now – always there to advise, manage my workload and diary and help to keep me organized.

My friends and publisher – Bluebird and One Boat books at Pan Macmillan and particularly Hockley – who, again, have become established as work colleagues and friends as they guide me through this, my seventh book.

My family and friends who understand that my work now is so important to me and especially to my 'him indoors', Tim, who reminds me daily that I am not getting any younger and the need to sometimes just put the brakes on a bit. I know he is right.

Last but by no means least – it is you the readers who have taken the time to read what I have to say, have invested in my books, given them as gifts and continue to spread the word. You are making your own changes too and that for me has to be the best outcome.

Thank you all.

ABOUT THE AUTHOR

Nancy Birtwhistle is a *Sunday Times* bestselling author, lifelong gardener and Hull-born baker who won the fifth series of *The Great British Bake Off* in 2014. Motivated by protecting the planet for her ten grandchildren, Nancy decided to change how she used plastic, single-use products and chemicals in her home. Sharing her tips online, she amassed an engaged international following of devoted fans interested not only in her delicious recipes, but also her innovative ideas and time-saving swaps that rethink everyday house and garden tasks to make as little an impact on the environment as possible.

Nancy worked as a GP practice manager in the NHS for thirty-six years until she retired in 2007. She lives in Lincolnshire with her husband, dogs and rescue hens. She is the author of *Clean & Green*, *Green Living Made Easy*, *The Green Gardening Handbook*, *The Green Budget Guide*, *Sizzle & Drizzle* and *Nancy's Green and Easy Kitchen*. *Clean Magic* is her seventh book.

Portrait by Mel Four.

INDEX

acidic cleaners 16, 18, 25–6, 29, 31–3, 43, 56, 64, 68, 76, 78, 116–18, 152–3, 182
   see also Pure Magic cleaner
acidic stains 25
acids 12, 16, 43, 45
   see also citric acid
Agas 97–101, 104
air fresheners 20, 177–8
algae 23, 28, 68–9, 72–4
alkaline cleaners 31, 78, 116–18, 152–3
alkalines 16, 43, 45, 56
All-purpose floor cleaner 19–20, 183
All-purpose spray cleaner 16–18, 20, 24–5, 43, 45, 109, 120, 131, 175, 183, 184
   recipe 10–11
aluminium 18, 23, 102, 107–8, 174
anti-bac 24, 33, 120, 134, 206, 222, 241, 253, 257, 274, 279
ants 25, 166, 199
astringents 270, 273
Avobenzone 247

babies, poosplosions 251–6
bacteria 26, 33, 120, 206, 237, 273–4
   see also anti-bac properties
baking powder 12
bananas 120
Basic Magic 13, 16–18, 20–3, 25, 29, 43–8, 56, 74, 78, 99, 173
   floor cleaner 47, 48
   kitchens 131
   recipe 44
   sinks 109, 110, 111
   slime stains 257–8
   stone bird baths 72
bathrooms 29, 30

baths
   acrylic 22
   cleaning 21–2, 27, 30, 47, 55
   taking 159–60
beeswax 133–8
best-before dates 131–2
BHT (butylated hydroxytoluene) 271–2
bicarbonate of soda 7, 18, 45, 78, 79–82, 84–5
   Cream cleaner 11–12
   Dry cleaning foam 60–3
   imitation grass 278
   kitchens 102, 104–6, 140, 146, 151–2, 154
   laundry 218–20, 225
   Liquid hand soap 265
   odour neutralization 150
   ovens 102, 104–6
   sinks 116, 117–18
   Sticky stuff paste 58–9
   wood marks 88
bin liners 160–1
bins 160–3
biodegradability 129
bird baths, stone 72–3
bird poo 47
biro stains 20, 35
black spot lichen 70–1
bleach
   chlorine 26, 31, 46, 65
   see also green bleach
blinds 170–2
blockages 93–122
blood stains 211
body odour 22, 238, 268–70
Body spray 15, 274–5
Bodywork solution 20, 174, 176–7
bowls, drinking/feeding 279

bread bags, wax 133
bronzer 245–51
bug stains 174, 175
bumps, on cars 175
burns/scorches 87, 90–1

carpets
    car 176–7
    moths 199, 230–1
    rust on 74, 76–7
    stains 20, 22, 35, 41, 57–9, 62, 74, 76–7, 256–8
carrier oils 185
cars 20, 30, 47, 173–8, 183, 237
cashmere 228
casserole dishes 104, 153
cats 232, 279
caustic soda 116
chickens 199–200
children 187, 212, 282
chocolate 20, 22, 45
Christmas 116, 145
chrome 26
cisterns 28, 51–4, 158
citric acid 7, 43, 56, 83–4, 117
    descaling kettles 27
    kitchen cleaning 152–4, 179
    Pure Magic 8–9, 26, 49, 53
citrus scents 13, 182–4, 239
cleaning products, home-made 2–20, 36–7
    see also specific cleaning products
cling film 1, 133
clothes horses 242–3
clothes moths 228–31, 235
clothing care 59, 193–260
    faded lines 244–5
    odour fresheners 223, 234, 236–8
    see also laundry
cloths 7, 32, 180, 224–5
    see also dishcloths
cloves 121–2
coats, woollen 217–21, 231
cobwebs 166–8
coffee grounds 113
coffee stains 33, 47, 221
composite 18–19, 32, 47
concrete 23, 70, 79, 82, 278
Conker detergent mark II 211–14
cooker aluminium filters 18
cooker hoods 18
cooking smells 237–8
copper 73, 139, 140
cotton 134–6, 207, 224, 228
Cream cleaner 11–13, 16–19, 25, 28–9, 33, 59, 79–80

car cleaning 175
chalky texture 12
kitchens 131, 146, 163
laundry 249–50, 259–60
leather upholstery 175
marks on wood 90–1
perfuming 13, 45
recipe 11–12
sinks 109
cream of tartar 12
cup rings 33, 87–9
cups 32, 47
curtains 234–5

dashboards 175
decking 68–70
decorating, preparation for 172–3
deep cleans 93–122
dental retainers 33
deodorant, home-made 15, 268–74
diatomaceous earth 198–200, 230
dishcloths 180, 224–5
Dishwasher detergent 151–4
dishwashers 48, 179
disinfectants 184
dogs 68, 95, 158, 167, 199, 277–9
doors 17, 19, 30
drains 111, 115
'dry clean only' items 218–21
Dry cleaning foam 59–63
Dry grease stain remover (Terre de Sommières/ Fuller's earth) 56–8, 90
dyes 225–6
    fixing 245

Easy-Breeze fabric spray 15, 20, 184, 227, 230, 234–8, 245
eco-friendly washing-up liquid 7, 56, 183, 205
    All-purpose floor cleaner 19–20
    Basic Magic 44, 45
    car cleaner 174
    Cream cleaner 11–12, 13
    Dry cleaning foam 60–1
    kitchen cleaning 146
    Liquid hand soap 265
    Oven Magic 99–100
    patio cleaner 69–70
    Pure Magic 8–9, 49, 53
egg shells 200
eggs, fried 140–2
emulsifiers 14–15, 185, 271, 275
enamel 98, 100, 153, 258
Epsom salts 159
erasers 83

essential oils 182–3, 232
  acidic 13, 45–6
  All-purpose floor cleaner 19–20
  All-purpose spray cleaner 10–11
  Basic Magic 44, 45
  Body spray 275
  car cleaner 174
  Cream cleaner 11–12, 13
  Easy-Breeze Fabric Spray 235–7
  and the environment 203
  General polish 15–16
  Home-made deodorant 270–4
  laundry detergents 204, 205, 208–9, 213–14
  Liquid hand soap 265–6
  non-acidic 13, 45–6, 265–6
  Pure Magic 8–9, 49, 53
  reed diffusers 185–6
  soap slivers 267–8
  see also specific essential oils
eucalyptus essential oil 46, 183, 201–2

fabric 57
  burns/scorches on 91
  rust stains 23, 27, 28
  see also clothing; upholstery
fabric softener 15, 167–70, 183, 200–3, 209, 217, 218–20, 222, 254
  perfuming 13
fast-fashion 196, 198
fats
  putting down sinks 112–13
  see also grease stains; oils
fertilisers 86
fire starters, orange peel 85
flies 119–22, 199
floor cleaners 19–21, 23, 45, 47–8, 56, 183
flour 112
food stains 25, 27–8, 33, 253
food waste 160, 162–3
freezers 145–50, 181, 276–7
fridges 63, 145–50, 181
fungicides 241
fur 228

garden tools 23, 27, 74, 76
gardening 86, 158, 159–60
general cleaning 18–20, 155–91
General polish 15–16, 20, 33, 89, 183
gifts 187–91, 231–4, 266–8
glass 17, 20, 24–5, 73, 79–80, 84–5, 106–7, 127–8, 131
glucose, liquid 14–16
granite 16, 22–3, 25–6, 28–9, 32–4, 43, 68

grass (imitation) 278
grease
  and sinks 112–13, 116
  stains 20–2, 25, 30, 45, 87, 90, 131, 172–3, 221–2, 249–50
  see also Dry grease stain remover
greaseproof paper 134–8
green, going 1–4, 16, 41, 281–3
green bleach (sodium percarbonate) 7, 18, 23, 30–3, 56, 64, 187
  black spot lichen 71
  blinds 171
  dishcloths 180
  Dry cleaning foam 59, 60–2
  kitchens 104, 108, 151–2, 163, 180
  laundry 218–25, 248, 254–7
  mop cleaning 165
  ovens 104, 108
  sheepskin rugs 169
  sinks 18–19, 109–11, 116
  stone bird baths 72
  wood marks 90–1
Green bleach foam 63–7, 146
'green washing' 129
greenhouses 73
grey water diverters 159–60
grout 20–3, 45, 47, 51
gutters 73

hand soap, Liquid 263–6
headlights 176
hobs 21, 29, 30, 153
holiday checklists 178–81
honey 14–16
hormone-disrupters 247
houseplants 70, 158, 180

ice makers 149–50
ink stains 20, 35
insect repellents 25, 119–22, 199
irons (steam) 88–9, 180
  Perfumed distilled ironing water 238–40
ivy 211
  Magic suds (ivy detergent) 215–17

jeans 225–6, 244
jewellery, tarnished 258–9
jumpers
  clothes moths 229–30, 231
  odours 237
  pilling 226–8
  washing 197, 198

kettles 27, 180
kitchen gadgets 125–6

kitchens 16–18, 29, 123–54, 162–3
knives 153

labelling 147, 148
lambswool fluffies 166–8
laminated wood 20
landfill 129, 164, 206–7, 252
laundry 193–260
    20°C cycles 206, 216, 218, 223, 242, 245, 249, 254, 257
    drying 242–3, 255
    hand washing 245
    holidays 180–1
    over-laundering 226–7
    pet bedding 277–8
    pilling 226–8
    pre-soaks 206, 221–2, 248, 254
    stains 8, 21–2, 27–8, 30–1, 34–5, 41, 45–7, 98, 143, 245–51, 256–8
    whites 28, 243, 248, 251
    see also fabric softener
laundry detergent 204–6, 211–17, 222–3, 242, 249, 254
    Liquid 204–6, 242, 249, 254
    perfuming 13
    see also Wool/delicates detergent
lavender 13, 46, 177–8, 230, 237, 239
    Lavender wand 231–4
leather 57, 175
Leidenfrost effect 141
lemon 24, 120–2, 149
    juice 45, 78, 117–18
lichen, black spot 70–1
lily pollen 34–5
limescale 7–8, 18, 26–7, 29, 34, 51, 83–4, 154, 200–1, 203, 217, 223, 238, 279
linen 228
litter trays 279
living rooms 20
loofahs 59

Magic Mixers 14, 15–16, 185–6, 201–2, 213–14, 235–6, 271, 275
Magic suds (ivy detergent) 215–17
makeup stains 20, 34–5, 47, 245–51
marble 23, 25, 26, 28–9, 57, 68
mattresses 59
medications 114
microplastics 7, 129, 242
mildew 26, 237, 241, 243
milk, freezing 181
mint 177–8
mirrors 20, 24
mop cleaning 164–6
moss 69

mould 8, 26, 32, 48, 63–5, 67, 73–4, 146, 171, 180, 241, 243
multi-surface cleaners 25

nail varnish 35
nappies 251–2
natural fibres 207, 228–9
    see also cotton; silk; woollens
neutralizing stains 78
non-acidic cleaners 11–13, 20–3, 25, 30, 34, 43, 45–6, 48, 63–7, 111, 116, 175
    see also Basic Magic; Cream cleaner; green bleach
non-acidic essential oils 13, 45–6, 265–6, 266
non-stick 102, 138–9, 140–2
nubuck 57

odours
    body 22, 238, 268–70
    clothing 223, 234, 236–8
    freezer 148–50
    neutralization 143, 150, 278
    pets 279
    room 237–8
    tobacco 237, 238, 245
    towels 240–3
oils 20, 22, 112–13, 131
orange peelings 85
outdoor furniture 28, 30, 73–4, 76
Oven Magic 19, 34, 80, 97–102, 105–6
ovens 17, 21, 29, 34, 97–107, 153
    aluminium filters 18, 107–8
    glass doors 79–80, 106–7
    shelves 97, 102–3

paint 35, 82, 115
paintwork 25, 47, 56, 76, 172
pans 104, 138–43, 153
pantries 129–33
paper 114
    packaging 127, 129
    wildflower seed 187–91
pasta 113
paths 23, 27, 68–70, 86, 143
patios 23, 68–70, 74, 74–5, 158
pavers 3, 23, 68–70
permanent marker 35
personal care 261–77
pets 261–3, 277–9
PFAS (per- and polyfluoroalkyl substances) 138
pH scale 43, 46, 86
pillow cases 59, 134
piping bags, reusable 133–8
plant pot marks 87–91
plastic bags 1, 2

plastics 164, 224
    burnt-on 17
    kitchen 126–7
    packaging 127, 129
    single-use 1–4, 160–1, 204, 282
    sticky 30
polyester 207
Polysorbate 80 14–16
poo stains 47, 62, 251–6
potash 86
power washers 68
product safety data sheets 236–7
pumice stones 79–87, 106, 226
Pure Magic cleaner 7–9, 16, 18, 26–8, 29, 43, 48–56, 65, 75–8, 80, 83–4
    black spot lichen 71
    crystallization 54
    gel 28
    kitchen cleaning 140, 142
    laundry 250
    mixing with alkaline cleaners 31
    neutralizing stains 78
    outdoor furniture 73–4
    overspray stains 56
    overspray stickiness 55–6
    pet bowl cleaner 279
    rust 75–6, 77, 131
    sandals/sliders 259–60
    shelf life 55
    sinks 109
    spray attachments 54–5
    tarnished jewellery 258–9
    toilets 181
Pure Magic Flush 51–4
Pure Magic Gel 49–51, 65, 76
PVC 23, 25, 30, 47, 73

quilts 59

rainwater 158, 238–40
red mites 199
reed diffusers 15, 20, 184–7
refreshes 93–122
rice grains 113
rosemary 177–8
rubber seals 32, 48, 63–7, 67, 109, 146
rugs, sheepskin 168–70
rust 8, 26–9, 74–7, 130–1, 166

salt 75–6, 76, 131, 272–4
sandals 259–60
sandalwood essential oil 13, 44, 46, 265–6, 271
saponins 211–12, 215
scaffolding 74–5

scarves 197
scratches 88, 175
seals, rubber 32, 48, 63–7, 67, 109, 146
seed, wildflower 187–91
sewers 111
sewing 211
sheepskin rugs 168–70
shelves, rust rings 76, 130–1
shoe polish 35
shoes 30, 82, 225–6, 238, 259–60
shower screen runners 28, 63, 67
showers 28, 29, 159
silicone 30, 63, 67
silk 22, 57–8, 221, 228, 231
silver 30
sinks 18, 21, 23–4, 27–30, 32, 55–6
    blockages 112–15
    ceramic 18–19
    composite 18–19, 32, 47
    daily cleans 47
    rust on 76
    slow-flowing 115–18
    stinky 3, 19, 109–11
skirting boards 25
slate 16, 20, 23, 25–6, 28–9, 32–4, 43, 48, 68
sliders 259–60
slime stains 22, 34, 256–8
slugs and snails 86
soap
    flakes 204–5, 207–9, 264–5
    Liquid hand 263–6
    Marseille unperfumed 204, 205
    slivers 266–8
soap scum 48, 116
socks 206
soft-top car roofs 176
sorbitan 14
spiders 166–8
spot cleaning 22, 220
Spot-cleaning solution 62
stainless-steel 18, 26, 138–43
stains 39–91
    see also specific stains
steps, slippery 68–70
sticky label residue 30, 59
Sticky stuff paste 58–9
stone 16, 20, 22–3, 25–6, 28–9, 32–4, 48, 57, 68, 70–6
stop taps 179
suede 57, 82–3, 225, 259
    faux 221
suede brushes 82, 225–6
sun cream stains 22, 27–8, 47, 245–51
sun parasols 28, 73
sunlight, bleaching effect 253

surgical spirit (rubbing alcohol) 34–5, 183
    All-purpose spray cleaner 10–11, 24
    carpet stain removal 20
    odour 24
    odourless 184, 235–6

taps 26, 51
tar 35
tarmac 68–70
tea leaves 113
tea stains 32, 33, 47
tea strainers 152–4, 183, 213, 215–16
tea towels 221–3
ticks 199
tights, strengthening 275–7
tile adhesive 82
tiles 23–4, 45, 47, 70
    encaustic 20, 22, 48, 80–1
    terracotta 80–1
tobacco odours 237, 238, 245
toilets 6, 26, 28, 51–4, 56, 78
    blocked 118–19
    cisterns 28, 51–4, 158
    and going on holiday 181
    pumice cleaner 83–4
    seats 19, 24
tomatoes 86, 87
tool kit, green cleaning 5–7
towels, fusty-smelling 240–3
toxins 2, 230, 235–7, 247, 271–2, 282
toys 30
trainers 30, 82, 225–6, 238, 260

underwear 197
upholstery
    cars 175
    fresheners 234–5
    leather 175
    stains 22, 35, 59, 62–3, 256–8
urine 62

vegans 14–15
vegetable glycerine 11–12, 66–7, 183, 201–2, 208–9, 265, 272–3
vegetables, grow-your-own 158
vinegar (distilled white) 7, 43, 56
    All-purpose floor cleaner 19–20
    All-purpose spray cleaner 10–11, 24
    Car cleaner 174
    Fabric softener 201, 202
    General polish 15–16
    infused 181–3, 203
    and kitchen cleaning 152
    and laundry 221, 244–5

    odour 24, 181
    and sinks 117–18
    Vinegar spray 63
    and washing machines 202–3
vodka 10–11, 184, 235–7
vomit 62, 237, 255

wall scuffs 22
walnuts 88
wardrobe refreshes 196–8
washing machines 32, 48, 63–5, 67, 179, 202–3, 210
washing soda (sodium carbonate) 7, 19, 23, 33–4, 43–4, 56, 64, 66–7, 69, 98–9, 205
    Basic Magic 44
    bins 161–2, 163
    blinds 171
    Dry cleaning foam 60–1
    kitchens 140, 143–4, 151–2, 163
    laundry 207, 217, 221–3, 225, 249, 253–7
    mop cleaning 165
    neutralizing stains 78
    ovens 99–100, 102–5, 108
    patios 69–70
    seized 143–4
    sinks 116, 117–18
washing-up liquid *see* eco-friendly washing-up liquid
waste 157–60, 160, 162–3, 196
water
    hard 152, 154, 223, 238
    soft 151–2
water marks 26, 28, 51, 72, 83, 87–9, 142, 171, 174, 225
water softeners 223, 253
water supply, turning off 179
water waste 157–60
white spirit 115
wildflower seed waste-paper gifts 187–91
windows 174
wine stains 25, 33
wipes, single-use 1, 114
witch hazel 268–74
wood ash 85–8
wood burners 84–5
wood, marks on 16–17, 20, 22–3, 28, 30, 48, 57, 78, 87–91
    see also decking
Wool/delicates detergent 167, 169, 206–11, 218–20, 227–8, 245
woollens 52, 197, 207–11, 217–21, 226–8, 231
work surfaces 16, 24, 26, 32–3, 153

xanthan gum 50, 66–7, 99–100, 102, 104–5, 265